Boswell's
Broadland

DUDLEY PUBLISHING

NORFOLK

2012

BOSWELL'S BROADLAND
First Published 2012

Dudley Publishing
1 Milebridge Farm Cottage
Spinks Lane
Wymondham
Norfolk NR18 0SR

A CIP catalogue record for this book is available
from the British Library

ISBN: 978-0-9565227-1-9

PRINTED IN GREAT BRITAIN
by Breckland Print, Norfolk

Contents

Acknowledgements 4

Foreword by Anthony Knights 5

The Artist 6

Introduction 8

Etchings and lithographs by other artists 10

Broadland Etchers and Lithographers in this book . .11

List of oil paintings 12

Locations map 13

Oil paintings and artist's diary 14–156

This book is dedicated to those
private individuals and Trust
members who help to conserve
and restore Norfolk's boating
heritage for future generations.

Acknowledgements

I would like to acknowledge and say a big thank you to all those who helped in the preparation and production of this book, in particular, Richard Barnes, for putting together a mountain of photographs, etchings and narrative and Nick Jermy for taking the photographs of the paintings. I don't know how they made sense of it all.

Christine spent literally days at the computer (she will say more) typing up my words, editing and correcting my terrible spelling and putting me on the path of common sense instead of indulging my romanticised and whacky viewpoints.

There was an army of kindly folk offering me boats to paint from which I am afraid I did not always accept; Liz and Bernard Bryan for Pug (MV), Ted and Marylin Brewster (dory), Glen Howarth for his Norfolk Reed Lighter, Patrick and Robin Richardson of Phoenix Fleet (dory), Ludham Marine Hirecraft to name just a few.

Many thanks to Anthony Knights, Commodore of the Royal Norfolk and Suffolk Yacht Club at Lowestoft for writing the foreword. He is a personal friend and altogether a very nice bloke. Many thanks also to Peter George for providing his archival material of early Broadland boatyard pennants and badges. Rachel Hipperson for her kind offer to give me access to the land she manages at Haddiscoe marshes. Nicola Hems, Curator, Museum of the Broads, for her help with archival references. Mrs. Rachael Card, Green book organizer for giving me permission to use various flags from the Green Book.

I am indebted to the following galleries who have handled my work s over the years; Tizzy Fairhurst of Fairhurst Gallery, Norwich, Andrew Wilson of A&K Galleries, Harpenden, Frames Gallery of St. Giles, Norwich, The Grapevine Gallery, Norwich , The Assembly Room, Norwich, Mandells Gallery, Norwich; Jorn Langberg of Langham Fine Art, Crome Gallery Norwich; Melinda Racker of Croxton Park, Thetford; Shepherd's Market Gallery, London; Robert and Daphne Dawson- Smith previously of The Saracen's Head, Wolterton; The Garden Gallery Southwold; Thompson's Gallery, Aldeburgh; The Mall Galleries, London, Ringstead Gallery of Burnham Market and The Flint Gallery, Blakeney.

The following list of books have proved invaluable in providing historical and factual details about Broadland artists, writers and photographers who lived and made reference to Norfolk's unique Broadland landscape;

British Artists working 1900-1950 by Grant M. Waters, *The Charmer of the Norfolk Broads* by C.A.Hannaford RBA, *How to Organise a Cruise on the Broads* by E.R.Suffling, *Broadland Illustrated* by G. Parsons-Norman, *Sun Pictures of the Norfolk Broads* by Payne Jennings, *A Guide to the Norfolk Broads* by W.A.Dutt, *Hathor: The story of a Norfolk Pleasure Wherry* by The Broads Authority, *The Battle of the Broads* by Martin Ewans, *The Wherryman's Way* by Steve Silk, *The Broads in Print* by David Clarke, *The Royal Norfolk and Suffolk Yacht Club* by Jamie Campbell, *Norfolk Broads: The Golden Years* by Phillipa Miller, *A Broad Canvas* by Ian Collins, *Broadland Sketches* by David Poole, *Wide Skies* by May and Watts and various books by Edward Seago including *A Canvas to Cover.*

The biggest thanks must go to the people I met on my amazing journey from holidaymakers wanting to know when the book would be published to boating people offering help and praise for my work. Without their help in tackling nearly two hundred miles of waterway my work would have been very difficult to complete. Last and by no means least, thanks to Paul Darley, fellow artist from Cromer, who accompanied me on my artistic journey from time to time and gave me encouragement to carry on.

Foreword

I think it may have been over an excellent lunch at the Royal Norfolk and Suffolk Yacht Club at Lowestoft (so splendidly painted by Patrick and also appearing in his admirable volume 'Boswell's Coast') that he first mooted the idea that I might like to write the foreword to his forthcoming volume: 'Boswell's Broadland'. We were at the club as I had suggested that he would perhaps be interested in helping me examine the club's collection of paintings and prints, all of course of a watery theme and I was not disappointed when he displayed his encyclopaedic knowledge of all things painterly with thoughtful insights into the club's Edward Seago and Frederick Cotman paintings.

Lunch over, the conversation meandered to the time, about 1959, that I first came across Patrick at the Norwich Frostbite Sailing Club when he asked me to crew him in his Enterprise dinghy 'Zuleika', in which, if my memory serves me correctly, we had considerable success. It is fascinating to consider that he started the current series of Broadland paintings, over fifty years later, but not much further up the river, at New Mills in Norwich and that a lovely painting of 'The Frostbites' appears early on in this book. Painting and sketching and out in all weathers, often in his Norfolk 14 ft dinghy 'Wings', he continued his Broadland journey down the River Wensum, thence into the River Yare, down to Breydon Water and then up the River Waveney, to the limit of navigation at Geldeston Lock. All the paintings reproduced in this volume were painted 'en plein air' and capture the spontaneity and freshness of his subjects as he directly perceives them from nature. I offer this insight merely to suggest that Patrick is continuing the fine tradition of Seago and Cotman along with other Norfolk painters of the waterside scene, such as Charles J. Watson (1846–1927) Charles A. Hannaford (1887–1972) and Charles M. Wigg (1889–1969) but in his own inimitable Norfolk impressionist style.

Patrick's 'Norfolk and Suffolk Odyssey' as it was becoming, continued on up to the northern rivers as they are collectively known, the Bure, Thurne and Ant, on all of which he has sailed in the many yachts, large and small that he has owned over the years. Within this volume you will also find delightfully captured, the fleeting essence of the principal Broadland Regattas, themselves also continuing the tradition started in the mid Victorian era and depicted by the many artists of the time. I am particularly fond of the scene at Acle Regatta, painted on the 21st of May 2011, as I was sailing on board 'Starlight Lady' that day and received a merry wave from Patrick as we sped past his retreat in the reeds, busy with his brushes.

What you have before you is truly a labour of love that I doubt could have been undertaken by any lesser mortal, the whole adventure taking over a year to complete. Patrick has travelled, winter and summer through the 200 miles of the entire Broads waterway system, setting up his easel, sketching, painting and making insightful notes on the often adverse conditions and of course the friendly and amusing comments of the ever inquisitive passerby.

I am extremely pleased and flattered that he has asked me to be a part, however small, of this extraordinary and illuminating exercise. Perhaps turning the pages here will kindle some desire in the reader to visit a few of the many delightful places so beautifully depicted in this volume.

Anthony Knights, January 2012
Commodore, The Royal Norfolk & Suffolk Yacht Club

The Artist

From an early age I was conscious that I had an artistic family background in that I learned about artists in my family. Aunt Faith was a portraitist who had paintings hung in the Stock Exchange in London. Aunt Ruth, an antique dealer, had her portrait painted as a young girl by A.J.Munnings. My sister Anne was an antique dealer and had a' good eye for pictures', as they say. My brother Roger too, was at one time training for architecture but ended up as a bomb disposal expert. The family thought that he would go out with a bang, but thankfully didn't before retirement.

It was further back in time that the family had a long association with the Norwich School of Artists, culminating with one of my forebears being made a Freeman of Norwich, something continued to this day with both male and female members of the family. My daughters Natalie and Sophie were among the first females to be inducted and swear their allegiance to be buxom to the Lord Mayor. The Freemen were originally carvers and gilders to Norwich artists and eventually would go on to have their own galleries in London Street run by Great Grandfather James and his brother Samuel. The family were the main agents

for A.J.Munnings in Norwich. At the turn of the 20th Century it was Major Bernard Boswell who continued the gallery as Boswell's in Tombland and I myself, latterly, ran Boswell's Fine Art from Orford Yard in Norwich for many years before taking up painting as a full time artistic occupation. I could wax lyrical about artists who influenced me, from Ken Howard to Bernard Dunstan, but I suppose like all things one goes back to early influences. Clara Leeds at Unthank College in Norwich, Mr. Robinson at Langley School and perhaps the biggest influence of them all, Mary Young, a retired lecturer in art from Hornsey College in London who gave me early encouragement from her studio in Southrepps.

Although painting and drawing were important to me all my life, my career path over the years has been diverse if nothing else. Trained originally as a classical French chef at Browns Hotel in London, my career led me to the Hilton Hotel, Royal garden Hotel and eventually to the South of France for further training at The Grand Hotel at Cap Ferrat, to the Hotel Juana, Juan Les Pins and finally to the Croix Blanche at Chamonix. Fluent French has helped me to direct tourists in Norwich on many occasions and in latter years found my way round a decent wine list if nothing else. Garden furniture design and property renovation too have been occupations that have taken my time over the years but it was always back to the paintings that kept my interest alive and I am sure it will continue to do so for many a year.

My first two books were of Norwich where I was born and bred, and the Norfolk and Suffolk Coast. This third book is of the beautiful landscape of Broadland that I have been sailing for almost sixty years.

Introduction

I can't tell you how much my Broadland journey meant to me as I indulged myself in travelling for the best part of a year through Norfolk's unique Broadland landscape. Vast dramatic skies and ever changing climate conditions were a constant revelation and never failed to please.

If it was not for my father being a bit of an old sea dog with his interest in boating and introducing his young family to the pleasure of just messing about in boats, it is unlikely I would have been so passionate about sailing and all things boats. From childhood to nearly in my seventies my love of boating has remained undiminished. As young children every summer weekend was spent at The Petersfield Hotel lagoon in Horning where he kept his pleasure houseboat *Arcadia* together with his sea going motor boat *Sea Girl*. The wherry provided parties galore with the war not long since over and a determination that people wanted to have fun and forget about that grey area of our history. He bought my first boat, an Enterprise I named *Zuleika* after the Cambridge siren who lured young undergraduates to an untimely demise in the River Cam. Sailing and attending regattas all over the Broads followed and I became a member of Horning, The Frostbites and The Norfolk Broads Yacht Clubs. For many of these old clubs the memberships are self perpetuating with sons and daughters following their parents lead. These sailing dynasties continue with the likes of the Brooms, Clabburns, Bentalls, Aitkens, Simpsons, Richardsons, Jeckells and Panks to name but a few. Their often vintage sailing boats lovingly restored and cared for help keep the Broadland yachting scene what it is today.

My journey through Broadland started in the centre of Norwich at New Mills down to Oulton Broad and Beccles and The Geldeston Locks Inn. Continuing back across Breydon Water and Yarmouth and up into the northern rivers. I was determined to visit the extremities of the rivers and went as far as West Somerton, Hickling and Heigham Sound. Up the Ant as far

as Sutton Staithe, Wayford and Dilham and then continued onwards to Wroxham visiting Salhouse, Ranworth until arriving at my final destination, Coltishall. I must confess the difficulties of painting in my little Norfolk dinghy. It had to be replaced by the inevitable car journey. I was pleasantly surprised at the access I achieved to get to suitable painting spots and didn't have far to carry my heavy painting equipment. A wheelbarrow, at one stage, was used. Not quite as bad as Stanley Spencer, the famous artist, who used an old pram. Mind you, he did wear pyjamas under his trousers so we can forgive him his eccentricity.

As an artist it goes without saying how I was influenced by previous Broadland painters, in particular in the Victorian and Edwardian eras. Stanley J. Batchelder's beautiful water colours of yachts and wherries, Charles M.Wigg's etchings and watercolours of the Broadland scene, Arnesby Brown of course who made his delicious paintings of Haddiscoe marshes and cattle his own. Through into the early part of the twentieth century I most admired Edward Seago's work painted from his beautiful Ludham home and Arthur Davies whose delightful watercolours are much admired today.

Perhaps the man who has influenced me and some young people today are still captivated by his books, is of course Arthur Ransome. Notably *Coot Club*, perhaps the most famous of his Broadland stories. There are legions of books mentioning The Broads since the 1920s when holidays afloat really started. Many of the original boatyards are still operating today.

I do hope you will find images of your favourite places with their own particular memories or indeed I may have rekindled your interest in wanting to visit new undiscovered parts of this wonderful Broadland landscape.

Patrick Boswell

above left: My father's boats, M.V. *Sea Girl* and wherry houseboat *Arcadia*
above right: Myself, my mother (on right) and my cousin in the 1950s
below left: My daughter, Natalie and her husband, James, with my wife's mother, Marjorie
below right: My wife, Christine

List of Etchings and Lithographs

C.M.Wigg 'Stokesby' (page 74)

 C.M.Wigg -possibly Hunsett (page 124)

C.M.Wigg – 'Wherry race, Barton Broad' (page 10)

C.M.Wigg 'Fishing match, Horning' (page 116)

etching above:
C.M. Wigg, WHERRY RACE BARTON BROAD

C.J.Watson 'Norfolk Marshes ' 1918 (page 68)

H.Percival (page 150)

H.Percival 'Harvesting' 1921 (page 138)

C.M.Wigg 1926 (page 150)

Frank Gillet 'Ratcatcher' (page 140)

Herbert Woods- (photo) Smuggler

C.M.Wigg 'A Norfolk Windmill' (page 102)

C.M.Wigg 'Beccles' (page 62)

H.J.Starling 'The Potter Heigham Bridge' 1889 (page 88)

C.M.Wigg Horning Ferry (page 142)

H.J.Starling 'Thurne Mill' (page 82)

C.J.Watson – July 14th 1888, Acle (page 128)

C.A.Hannaford 'Master Mariners' (page 148)

C.M.Wigg 'Acle Regatta' 1927 (page 42)

C.M.Wigg 'A Norfolk Windmill' (page 72)

C.J.Watson 'Low Tide Yarmouth' May 1894 (page 70)

C.M.Wigg 'Barton Broad' (page 134)

C.M.Wigg (page 76)

H.W.Tuck 'The Tannery' (Riverside, Norwich) (page 20)

C.J.Watson 'Boat building on the Yare' 1879 (page 52)

H.Percival 1912, Wherryman and his wife (page 96)

H.Percival 1907, A.J.Banhams boatyard, Horning. (page 114)

H.Percival (page 44)

C.A.Hannaford 'Starshell' (page 30)

Broadland Etchers and Lithographers included in this book

Charles J. Watson R.E. (1846–1927)

Painter and Etcher of landscapes and architectural subjects. He worked extensively in Norfolk and lived in Norwich and later in London. He was married to the artist Minna Bolingbroke.

Charles Mayes Wigg (1889–1969)

Landscape painter in oil and water colour. Born in Nottingham and educated at Gresham's School, Norfolk. Served in World War I and was wounded at Gaza. As a result he was invalided out of the army. He worked mainly in Norfolk and had a studio at Brundall. Later he moved to Barton Turf.

Charles Arthur Hannaford RBA (1887–1972)

Landscape painter in watercolour who studied under Stanhope Forbes the Newlyn School artist. Educated and studied art in Plymouth. He lived in London and Norfolk. Best remembered locally for running Broads Tours from Wroxham whose boats influenced his pictures. He published a book entitled *The Charm of the Norfolk Broads.*

Henry James Starling RE (1805–1996)

A Norwich man who lived in Bracondale and worked for many years at Colman's printing works as works director. Studied under Charles Hobbis and Horace Tuck. He taught himself lithography and etching and was best known for etchings of Norwich and Broadland. He was Chairman of Norwich Art Circle and a Governor of Norwich School of Art.

Frank Edward Gillett RI (1874–1927)

Painter in oil and watercolour of landscape and sporting subjects, illustrator and etcher. He was born at Worlingham in Suffolk and educated at Greshams in Norfolk. He worked at The *Daily Graphic* and illustrated sporting and dramatic subjects and became a member of The Langham Sketch Club. Lived at Aldeby, Norfolk and Beccles, Suffolk.

Harold Stanley Percival ARE (1868–1914)

A marine painter elected to the Royal Society of Painter-Etchers and Engravers in 1905. Born at Bickley in Kent on the 6th Sept 1868, he followed a career as an engineer until 1897 and was involved in the construction of the Manchester Ship Canal. He worked as an artist in Sussex and East Anglia.

Oil paintings

1. New Mills, Norwich
2. Coslany Bridge
3. Petch's Corner
4. Carrow Bridge
5. Thorpe Green
6. Frostbites Sailing Club
7. Marshman's Cottage, Postwick
8. Princess Elizabeth, City Boats
9. Bramerton Woods End
10. Surlingham Ferry
11. Coldham Hall Regatta
12. Wheatfen Home Dyke
13. Rockland Broad
14. Beauchamp Arms, Buckenham
15. Acle Regatta
16. Langley Dyke looking towards Cantley
17. Loddon Staithe
18. Thurne Regatta
19. Reedham Ferry Inn and Crossing
20. Reedham and Reedham Swing Bridge
21. St Olaves Bridge
22. (narrative only- Three Rivers Race)
23. Somerleyton Swing Bridge
24. Oulton Broad and Wherry Hotel
25. Royal Norfolk & Suffolk Yacht Club and basin
26. Beccles River View
27. The Locks Inn, Geldeston
28. Berney Arms Mill and PH
29. Breydon Water
30. Yarmouth Yacht Station with North-West Tower
31. Stracey Wind Pump, Acle New Road
32. Stokesby Staithe
33. Acle Bridge Inn
34. Wroxham Regatta
35. Upton Dyke
36. Thurne Dyke
37. Beccles Regatta

38. Horning Regatta
39. Potter Heigham Bridge
40. Sea Week, Lowestoft
41. Somerton Staithe
42. Heigham Sound
43. Waxham New Cut
44. Hickling Village Regatta
45. The Hickling Pleasure Boat Inn
46. Horsey Staithe
47. Womack Broad
48. Oulton Regatta Week
49. St Benet's Abbey
50. Ludham Bridge
51. Barton Regatta
51A. (Barton – Bank Holiday Monday narrative only)
52. Cox's Boatyard, Barton Turf
53. The Swan Inn Horning and Wherry Albion
54. How Hill
55. Irstead Shoals
56. Neatishead Village
57. Wayford Bridge
58. Dilham Tonnage Bridge
59. Sutton Staithe
60. Museum of the Broads
61. Hunter's Fleet, Womack
62. The Wherry Trust, Ludham
63. Hunsett Mill
64. South Walsham Broad
65. Ranworth Staithe
66. Horning Ferry Inn
67. Salhouse Broad
68. Hoveton Little Broad
69. Wroxham Bridge
70. Wherry Yacht Charter trust base
71. Belaugh Village
72. Coltishall Village Green
73. Wherries Yarmouth bound (front cover)

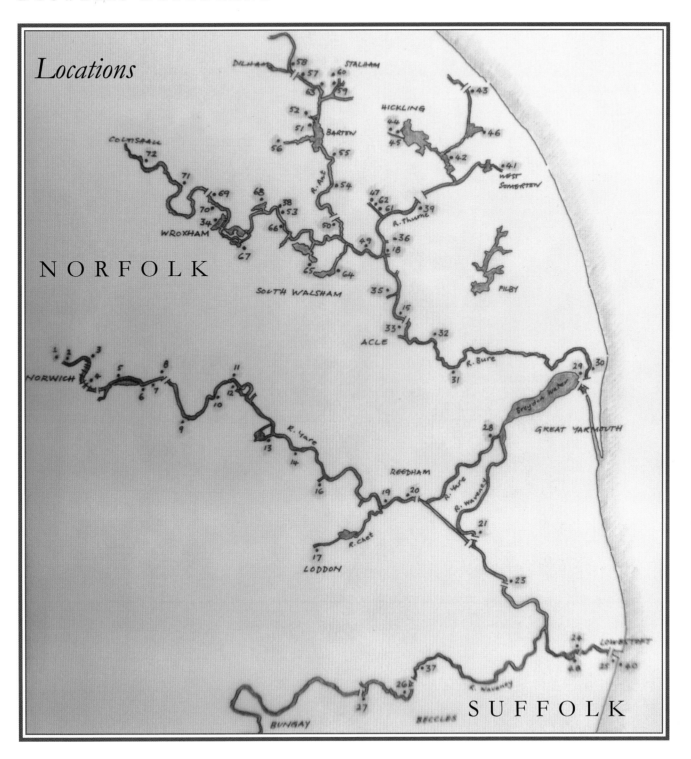

Locations

March 8th 2011

Viewed *The Dude* motor boat at Johnson's yard, St Olaves.

March 11th 2011

Returned for second viewing of *The Dude* with Christine this time. She seemed to like it but I fear she has a different agenda to me as I see the boat as a mobile artist's studio not an interior design project. We shall see who wins. Awaiting engine testing before I make a decision.

Engine turned out to be on its last legs. Abandoned ship.

Wednesday March 23rd 2011

1. New Mills, Norwich

Oil on board, 11.5" x 9"

After a drastic rethink about *The Dude* I have put my boating journey down to my trusty Norfolk dinghy *Wings*, no B4. With the purchase of a small electric engine from Norfolk Yacht Chandlers of Wroxham, I set out with high hopes on a beautiful sunny day, for Norwich to start my Broadland adventure. There is a very steep slipway on Friar's Quay and I soon had *Wings* launched with a secure rope wrapped around a nearby stanchion, together with passer-by Gary, a youth worker, dragged from enjoying the sun on some nearby steps, who assisted.

Some might question starting my trip from Norwich but I really wanted to begin at New Mills Yard, the extent of navigation for small boats on the Wensum. I quietly slipped by abseiling window cleaners on the Art School building and passed effortlessly under the Sir John Soane bridge, Duke Street bridge, and finally Coslany bridge by the old Bullards Brewery building. It was fascinating to see these bridges that I was so familiar with from my new watery perspective. Some dappled water with just the occasional duck and seagull for company. The road traffic was just a distant murmur with only the City Hall clock to break the silence in the background.

A quick jettisoning of my mud-weight mid-stream and I was soon engrossed painting my subject. Lunchtime beckoned and I rang my daughter Natalie who works at The Castle Museum, for a trip down the river. The last time she made this journey to New Mills she was just a toddler in my old gaff rigged sailing cruiser *The Smuggler*. Though she did not thank me for it, later on she managed to get blue paint on her hands and dress. Oh dear, naughty Daddy!

I shall endeavour to paint or at least sketch the remainder of the Norwich bridges. There is so much history here from the Viking invaders, led by Sweyn who reached this part of the city. Later the Norwich School of painters depicted the everyday working life of the river from New Mills all the way to Whitlingham and Postwick Grove. From Crome and Cotman to Stannard and Ninham , not forgetting my own favourite Charles J. Watson's evocative watercolour of Fye Bridge with just a hint of figures and wagons passing over the top of the bridge. So many of these bridges have been replaced or swept away in the Victorian floods and their replacements tell their own particular story.

1. New Mills, Norwich

~ *Boswell's Broadland*

2.Coslany Bridge

Oil on board 11" x 9"

Location; At anchor downstream from centre of river
Weather; Another glorious sunny day with a slight breeze

Today was a depressing start as I stupidly launched *Wings* myself without seeking assistance. Down she went and even with a double turn around a nearby stanchion, it wasn't enough to stop her momentum. She hit the water with a CRASH and threw the attached outboard into the water. Luckily, I quickly retrieved it and, miracle upon miracle, it started first time. It was a bit like yesterday when I motored back to the slipway with a mudweight still dragging along the riverbed. Call yourself a sailor?!

The rest of the morning went brilliantly with the EDP photographer turning up to take photographs of some mad bloke trying to paint from a small dinghy. Still, with my Danish flag flying from the masthead, a wink and a nod to Norwich bound Viking invaders, hopefully this should be enough to see off any more disasters.

2. Coslany Bridge

~ *Boswell's Broadland*

Tuesday 29ᵗʰ March 2011

3. Petch's Corner

Oil on board 12" x 10"

Location ;Adjacent to Zak's restaurant and opposite the Cow Tower.

Weather; A warm and sunny day

After receiving permission to paint next to Zaks I was in the process of setting up my easel but bumped into Cedric Copping who had come to inspect the old wherry mast erected nearby on behalf of The Norwich Society. His family business, Cushion & Co timber merchants, used to tow lighters of timber up the river through Norwich, to their yard. They could possibly have been traditional wherries but he has no record of it.

The bend of the river here is steeped in history. The Cow Tower on the far bank was used to fortify the city and duplicates another such structure called the Devil's Tower below Bracondale. Adjacent to me is the aforementioned wherry mast which denotes the spot where wherries were repaired at Petch's Yard. I remember, as a boy, it was the boat house for the police patrol launches. Zaks itself is built on the site of the old city mortuary. A passer-by told me a story of a man who broke into the mortuary one night and committed suicide thus saving his family the trauma of him ending his days at home. How considerate and how shocking.

A brisk walk along the river to The Red Lion at Bishop's Bridge, where the landlady kindly said I could launch *Wings* from her slipway, if I so wished. Waved to Janet Hepworth as she drove by looking 'tres elegant'. I looked like an old tramp in my painting gear.

I went to the doctors this morning, who for some bizarre reason, measured me. I seem to have lost ¾" in height. Ah well, being only 6' 2" is no bad thing. I wish!

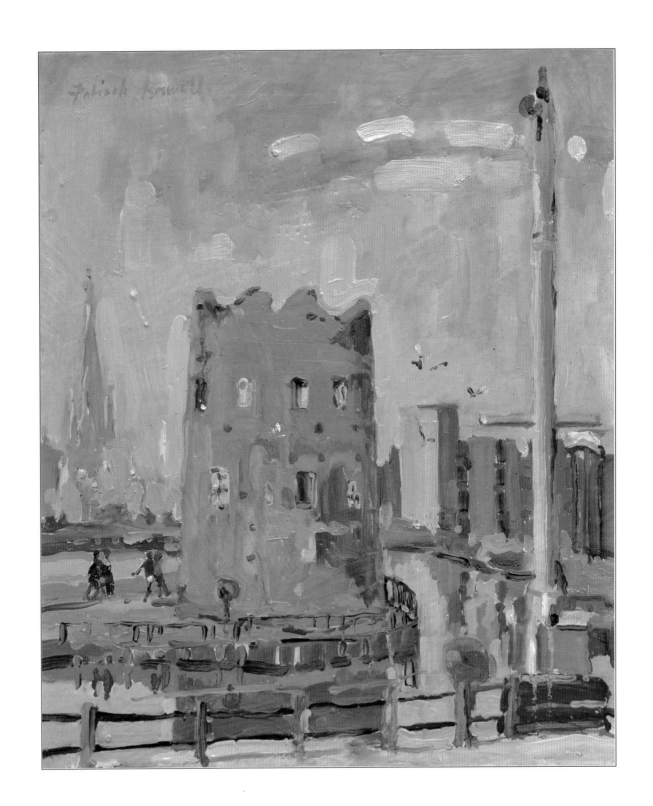

3. Petch's Corner

~ *Boswell's Broadland*

4. Carrow Bridge

Oil on board 11" x 9"

Location; Downstream of Carrow Bridge opposite Colman's factory. Adjacent to Norwich City's football ground.

Weather; A rainy start first thing but gradually drying and becoming drier by midday. Wind strong to gale force.

After last weeks' disaster with *Wings* I thought it couldn't get any worse. How wrong I was. Painting was going reasonably well until a violent gust of wind caught my easel, smashing it against the riverside quay heading and pitching its' contents, including the painting, oil paints, brushes and palette into the water. Luck would have it that the wind held most of the contents from floating away. So with a stick, one by one, I retrieved most things including my very soggy felt trilby. Alas all the oil paints, about £50 worth together with linseed oil bottles went to Davey Jones' locker.

By this point I was in a state of shock so went for a brisk walk to collect my thoughts. I wasn't to be beaten and in due course carried on, shaken but not stirred.

Lunch was called for so I decamped to 'The Yellow Room' at the football ground. Not bad really but could have done without background music from the sixties. It made me feel very old. I found myself tapping away to Helen Shapiro's 'Like a rubber ball, come bouncing back to me'. Pretty apt for a football team. It must be nearly 40 years since I last visited Norwich's ground. My sister Anne married into the Sands' family and her father-in-law, Hubert, I believe was a director, if not, Chairman at one time. The family interest is continued with Daniel Sands on the supporters committee.

H.W. Tuck
THE TANNERY, Riverside Road, Norwich

4. Carrow Bridge

~ *Boswell's Broadland*

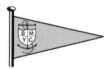

5. Thorpe Green

Oil on board 12" x 9"

Location; Thorpe Green, opposite the old Hearts Cruisers boat yard and facing The Rushcutters

Weather; Sunny morning but it had clouded over by lunchtime. Wind- light to moderate

The painting went well this time and I was able to reflect on my surroundings. So many memories of this area. The Buck PH, Jim Cole's house facing the river, Chaplin and Farrant's architect's office close by where Christine first started work.

Facing The Rushcutters, formerly named 'The Boat and Bottle' and as I remember it as a lad 'The Thorpe Gardens' where you could get a late drink on a Saturday night if you travelled out of the city's early closing restrictions. Ten deep at the bar and every man for himself, those were the days.

Further along the river stands the Town House Hotel. Managed by a young Robert Dawson-Smith in the sixties, notorious now as the last resting place of one of the Kray twins.

Thorpe Green and the river are steeped in history and the one time derelict Thorpe Old Hall is now beautifully restored. Joseph Stannard's fabulous painting 'Water Frolics' and an unfinished work by Cotman, both of this area, hang at the Castle Museum.

There is also a legend that on Thorpe island opposite my viewpoint, where the railway runs, the cries of the injured can be heard on a particular night of the year, near where a terrible rail crash took place in Victorian times with major loss of life.

Last of all it was a sad day when the old MTB owned by Commander Ashby, who lived aboard, was removed from Thorpe Green. He ran the old Hearts Cruiser site close by with his son Vaughan, who to this day carries on his father's tradition of running boat fleets both in London and on the French canals.

The green itself has many memorial seats dedicated, I noted to one June Arnison, a noted ceramicist, and to Chic Applin whom I knew well as the resident band leader at The Norwood Rooms Banqueting Suite in Norwich. I managed the bars and he played 'Lily the Pink' to a thousand revellers a night.

5. Thorpe Green

~ *Boswell's Broadland*

6. Frostbites Sailing Club, Norwich

Oil on board 12" x 10"

Location;Opposite bank to Frostbites sailing club and adjacent to Whitlingham, Broad's foot-path.

Weather; Sunny day first thing but clouding over by lunchtime. A brisk wind.

It was a hard choice whether to launch Wings at the Frostbites with all the hard work that that entails on my own or to tramp around Whitlingham Broad from the visitors Centre. I opted for the latter with its' thirty minutes of walking carrying my painting gear. No mean feat. I don't mind saying the reward far outweighed the effort with the New Cut on my left and the Broad on my right sparkling in the sunlight. It really is a haven for wildlife at this time of the year and I was lucky to have the path to myself with my early start.

I learnt a lot from the information boards en route as I passed by ;the confluence of the rivers Yare, Tas and Wensum; the bridge where the railway accident happened in 1874 killing 27 people, Norfolk's worst railway accident as I mentioned before. Something I didn't know was that in 1929 Norfolk's own Woodhenge was discovered with its circle of tree trunks surrounded by two ditches close by. Seahenge eat your heart out. The Romans were known to have settled here later because of its important link to Caistor St. Edmund and the river here giving it access to the North Sea. Trowse Eye gave us the named island close by.

Looking back from the Frostbites towards Carey's Meadow at one time was the old Norwich power station immortalised in a lovely winter scene by Edward Seago.

Winter is the reason that the Frostbites sailing club exists and has a vigorous sailing programme mainly sailed in traditional Norfolk dinghies these days. As a young lad I sailed my Enterprise dinghy *Zuleika* here, cracking the ice on the river and sailing in the snow. This was not for the fainthearted. I have fond memories of old club stalwarts such as Chamberlain, Aikens and Bentall, all now long since gone. The spirit of the club still carries on and is rigidly proud of being the oldest winter sailing club in the country. Sadly, on the day of my painting there was no sailing but a few Norwich School rowing club members came sculling through to liven up the scene.

6. Frostbites Sailing Club

~ *Boswell's Broadland*

7. Marshman's Cottage, Postwick

Oil on board 10" x 8"

Location; On the bank opposite to the old May Gurney's yard but now operated by the Broads Authority
Weather; Dull but brightened up by mid morning. Quite warm with no breeze.

The trip down Whitlingham Lane is always a pleasure, past Norwich Ski Club and the new Whitlingham Broad. I have fond memories, as a boy, cycling down here from the City to dig in the old Victorian dump for bottles to collect or sell on. The lane itself was a favourite haunt for the Norwich School painters , being just outside the City. J.J. Cotman painted the area repeatedly with his trade mark distant blue trees.

Although the area has been crimped and tidied to a certain extent by the various authorities, it still hasn't lost a lot of it's natural beauty with its' abundant wildlife. On the way I stopped to admire a wooden statue, by Mark Goldsworthy, on the river bank. A figure of a man which had been slightly vandalised. Pity really.

My eventual painting spot was a stopping place at the end of the lane where I took the river path alongside a nature reserve. Seeing only one man and his proverbial dog, who moaned about the parking area, now barriered off by the Broads Authority. I suppose it is to protect the wildlife but with four trail bikers screaming through it at one point it seemed a pointless exercise.

The marshman's cottage that I painted was at one time isolated and served the occupier well as he cut sedge and reed from the marshes. Today it is a Listed Building having been beautifully restored by May Gurney who at one time considered knocking it down. It stand rather forlornly today amongst the plethora of Broads Authority dredgers and machines. To the left is a small boat house, home to what I always call a river commissioner's launch but now run by the Broads Authority. I wonder what their title is, Broads Rangers perhaps? One such gave a wave as he passed by, as did most of the hire cruisers. I suppose it's the old bloke on the bank who took their attention.

The upstream river housed a few riverside cottages. One called Yare View was very smart indeed. I have a feeling it was a past mooring place for Bernard Matthews' sea going motor cruiser.

I wouldn't say that this is a quiet spot with the voluminous traffic noise from the motorway behind me and on the other side of the river, trains passing up and down twixt Norwich and Yarmouth. However I did see some wildlife with a heron gently gliding towards me and settling nearby. They never fail to delight the eye.

7. Marshman's Cottage, Postwick

~ *Boswell's Broadland*

8. Princess Elizabeth, City Boats

Oil on board 11" x 9"

Location;On the bank of Sheerline motor Cruisers facing City Boats yard.

Weather; Warm and dry first thing. Beautifully sunny by lunchtime.

Peter Applegate kindly let me stand on his land to paint the *Princess Elizabeth*. Here lay a few of those lovely old Broads Tours boats emanating from Wroxham. I painted the *Elizabeth* and in the distance, *Vanguard*.

I am reminded of C.A. Hannaford, the Broadland artist, who illustrated these touring boats in his little booklet 'The Charm of the Norfolk Broads'. *Princess Margaret*, known as 'the children's boat', *Princess Mary, Marchioness, Marina,* and *Her Majesty* named by Lady Delia Peel in 1950. *Princess Anne* and *Princess Alexandra* followed later. These beautiful passage boats still ply the Broads from Wroxham and Norwich though I must confess I have never travelled on one.

I think with a lovely subject like this I am inspired to paint freely and respond in kind to the subject with a pleasing result.

8. Princess Elizabeth, City Boats

~ *Boswell's Broadland*

9. Bramerton Woods End

Oil on board 10" x 8"

Location; One hundred yards upstream from the Woods End pub.

Weather; At last a glorious period of sunshine. Just a light South-Easterly blowing.

I drove to Bramerton today for the first time in many years. Unfortunately I am so out of date that I didn't realise the road through Trowse has been cut off and turned into mini housing areas. It is quite well done but this meant a quick detour to get back on track.

Arriving at The Woods End always comes as a surprise with the road twisting and turning through narrow lanes. On arrival I had the place to myself and tried the crank-up tourist recording for visitors, telling us about Billy Bluelight who made a living running along the path of the Yare from Norwich to Yarmouth for wages. Quite a feat in Edwardian times with no fancy hard edged paths to follow. A delightful large statue of him stands nearby.

The painting was done *contre jour* which is how I like to paint. The sun rippled on the water and the silence was only broken by the occasional passing boat with early holiday makers and squabbling pairs of geese flying down river.

There did not seem much sign of life at the pub although I did start at 8.30am. The early artist catches the scene. I noted with interest, a slipway for *Wing*s which may come in handy at a later date.

C. A. Hannaford
'STARSHELL'

9. **Bramerton Woods End**

~ *Boswell's Broadland*

10. Surlingham Ferry

Oil on board 14" x 8"

This mornings' painting went so well that I was encouraged to go quickly to Surlingham Ferry which is not far. The ferry itself has not functioned since the sixties but the landlady Sonia Cox at the adjacent Ferry House was very helpful in allowing me to paint on her land.

I positioned my easel looking back at the pub and had for company a man repairing the pathways by the quayheading. The car park was packed with walkers who would return at lunch time later on. They stood for a group photo in front of my painting but did not quite block out the view. On the far bank a police car pulled up and let two dogs loose in the water, practising recovery I suppose. On this bank it was quiet except for one boat mooring up which I had noted in my scene. However, later a boisterous crowd of jolly boat hirers moored in front of me but they were quite friendly shouting instructions on how to moor properly. They displayed the 'jolly Roger' from the boats' stern. I was very impressed that all the kids had lifejackets on.

Tony Knights left a message about paintings from the Royal Norfolk and Suffolk Yacht Club to be examined. I will ring when I return.

10. Surlingham Ferry

~ *Boswell's Broadland*

11. Coldham Hall Regatta

Oil on board 14" x 9"

Location; I drove to the furthest point opposite the Coldham Hall pub and sat on the small jetty that is not in private ownership.

Weather; Continual sunshine today with the driest April for years. Wind quite strong from the North-East.

Today was always going to be a bit of a push so I did not take my painting gear, just sketch books and painting seat. My jetty position took in the dinghy park, pub and Coldham Hall starting box so I had a really good view and was able to do various drawings with one on to a gesso panel. I had just enough time to record a little bit of the allcomers race and saw John and Caroline Ellis in B70 leading the Norfolk contingent, followed by Wendy Bush crewed by Pat Woodcock. Whether they saved their time against a large fleet of Yeomans remains to be seen. Tomorrow is the last day of the regatta so I will have to return another day to complete my painting.

I spoke to only one man with his dog who was disappointed when I told him he would have to drive to Norwich and back to reach the pub. I have spent a lifetime trying to navigate myself there over the years so didn't endeavour directions for such a challenging place to find. If you find him still out there ask him in for a cup of tea.

(continued Monday 9th May) I returned to finish my painting, following a delightful Sunday wedding of my friend's daughter Isobel Morton getting married to Sam. At any rate the weather continued apace and after parking, by kind permission of Eastwoods Boatyard, Brundall, I was soon painting furiously. I only managed to lose one thing in the water today, my molestick.

A boat from a local yard had decided to do a photo shoot from the same spot as me which made it a bit cramped in such a confined spot. The photographer didn't apologise for inconveniencing me and I was glad when they went.

Coldham Hall, being the first of the Broadland Regattas brought back happy memories of boyhood sailing here with the likes of Tom Percival, Alan Mallett and others attending. The weekend before Coldham Hall is usually the last downriver race from Norwich Frostbites Sailing Club. Tom Percival, in years gone by, gained an advantage by cutting the corner through Surlingham Broad to win the race whilst everyone else took the traditional river route. Each year now, at the pre-race meeting, Tom's corner cutting is forbidden thus ensuring his name lingers on to this day in the sailing instructions.

11. Coldham Hall Regatta

~ *Boswell's Broadland*

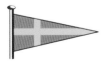

12. Wheatfen (Home Dyke)

Oil on board 10" x 8"

Location; The Ted Ellis Foundation adjacent Wheatfen Broad.

Weather; yet again another sunny day. Don't hold your breath.

On arriving at the Foundation I rang John Ellis who appeared as if by magic from the visitor's learning centre that he is helping to complete. We stood talking to each other on our mobiles only yards apart. John, although busy, was just brilliant giving me a lightning trip of possible painting sites and then left me to my own devices. His warden, David Nobbs, was also helpful and loaned me a wheelbarrow to take my gear to a good spot. This place is truly remarkable with its broadwalk access to a thatched viewing building to observe the wildlife. Home Dyke, where I set up my easel, was so tranquil a place and I only saw two other people in all my time there. David, the warden, told me that the Swallowtail butterfly was a week early this year because of the weather but it was quite worrying as the marshland flowers were not yet in bloom to provide foodstuffs.

On returning to the centre's buildings I was introduced to the local vicar, John Shaw, whose wife Wendy runs a contemporary art space at Rockland St. Mary. They do free breakfasts once a week. I had better not tell my starving artist friends about this one.

After painting I called in at John and Caroline's house for coffee and sandwiches. Yum Yum. Caroline recently retired from the Castle Museum where she was a museum registrar. My daughter Natalie also works there as a display co-ordinator. Their house really is delightful and I was given a guided tour by John who proudly showed me framed art works completed in wool by his grandmother. The detail is quite remarkable.

Keen to show me the area, John took me for a brisk walk across the marshes which are close to Coldham Hall PH and I subsequently spoke to the landlord and his wife tending the grounds. I admired John's sailing cruiser *Stratos* lying in the dyke. Then it was onward to pay a visit to Henry Fillery who runs his boat restoration business adjacent to the pub. I admired John's old boat *Blue Jacket* bequeathed to him by Beryl Wilberforce- Smith and now in the capable hands of John and Caroline's son Matthew. The boat sheds were run by Harry Last known for many a year as running the pub too.

John's guided tour of the area and encyclopaedic knowledge were just brilliant to listen to. However, don't get into a maths contest with him, you will lose.

Just as an after thought, I was priviledged to view and sketch the original Wheatfen house. The cottage, which is totally secluded and surrounded by carr and woodland, and must have been a great playground for the young John and his siblings to grow up in. His abiding memory of it was how cold it was in winter.

12. Wheatfen
Home Dyke

~ *Boswell's Broadland*

Wednesday 18th May 2011

13. Rockland Broad

Oil on board 16" x 8"

Location; Painted from inside the Rockland hide.

Weather; A dull day with a light southwest wind. Sunnier after 12 noon.

Having learned my lesson from Wheatfen's visit I brought my trusty garden wheelbarrow along this time. Just as well as leaving the Rockland St. Mary Staithe until you reach the hide is a good mile in distance. It was quite lovely with glimpses of the broad to my left and grazing marshes to the right. The path is called the Wherryman's Way and indicates where the old trading wherries would cross the broad from the main river to load up with marsh hay, reed, and timber for export. The broad is also the last resting place for wherries over the years with their long wooden bones sticking out of the water at low tide.

It was quite fun painting inside the hide, just like a studio really though it proved quite difficult to paint sitting down as the bench seats couldn't be adjusted. My task was soon done and as usual the light and weather improved as soon as I had finished.

Returning to the staithe I read with interest about 'old Scientific Fuller', a 19th Century wildfowler who lived in a houseboat close by. The old photograph of his boat shows his punt for wildfowling moored up and his eel nets for repair or drying alongside.

I made a detour on my journey home to Coldham Hall to take photographs inside Henry Fillery's boatshed but was too late to catch *Blue Jacket* before she was launched. Met up with John and Caroline Ellis and helped them to take the boat to its moorings and to step its mast. Bill for hernia op in the post.

The sailing boat *Sophie* inside boatshed at Coldham Hall

13. Rockland Broad

~ Boswell's Broadland

14. Beauchamp Arms, Buckenham

Oil on board 14" x 12"

Location; Painted downstream from Buckenham Sailing Club looking towards the Beauchamp Arms

Weather; Sunny day with virtually no cloud or wind base

I am getting quite used to the Rocklands now with its' broad and winding roads, on through Claxton and detouring off for the Beauchamp Arms. This is a building that I am quite familiar with as I passed it frequently in *Smuggler* on the Yare Navigation race. Actually from my viewpoint on the bank the pub looked delightful silhouetted against the distant horizon. The other direction highlighted Cantley sugar beet factory which I will tackle later. With the sun beating down my task was soon complete broken only by the occasional floating palace style boats drifting up from Brundall Marina. Apart from the landlord of the pub I spoke only to Paul Wright, the boat builder who gave me permission to park close to his yard.

I can tell that I am getting close to Langley and my old school as one of the school's houses was named Beauchamp like the pub. The Beauchamps were wealthy landowners centuries back. On that note –' home James and don't spare the horses'.

14. Beauchamp Arms, Buckenham

~ *Boswell's Broadland*

C. M. Wigg 1927
ACLE REGATTA

15. Acle Regatta

Oil on board 14" x 8"

Location; Upstream 200 yards on opposite bank from regatta tent and starting line

Weather; Brilliant sunny day with strong winds increasing by lunchtime. Force 4-5 increasing

There is something about a regatta that generates excitement especially when the weather and winds are good. Acle lived up to its reputation in bucket loads with a good 15 river sailing cruisers arriving in the morning with their attendant motorised mother ships towing them. These days, of course, the yachts themselves have their own inboard, feathered propped engines to get them out of trouble on a lee shore.

I left my car at the Bridge Store car park and attempted to proceed upstream with all my painting gear. The river bank was blocked off at one point because of a massive drainage channel that they are building but I was able to cross this at one point. I had visions of sinking into its muddy bottom but luckily this was baked hard. Because of the strength of the wind I took shelter between the river reed beds and the new high bank to protect the marshes from flooding. It was a surprisingly calm spot but left me with limited views of the boats' hulls and occupants. The scene did not disappoint as the yachts set off in staggered starts so I was able to get a second look at the subject, so to speak, with my painting. Even Tony Knights managed to give me a wave as he sailed past.

A superb scene and it is a credit to the sailors who seem firmly in control being well reefed. Even little *Blue Jacket* who had come up from Coldham Hall and was going great guns. It has been a lovely day and I am glad that I broke my painting journey on the Yare to attend. No doubt this will be one of many excursions I shall make as I continue my artists' journey.

 P.S. I won the Ebbage Cup here with *Smuggler* many years ago.

P.P.S A group of youths on a hire cruiser, evidently quite 'happy' started shouting at me as they passed, relating to my age and what I was doing. Being a perfect gentleman I gave them the victory salute for Agincourt which seemed to make things worse. I hadn't really thought about the consequences, that they might turn around and chase me up the bank. Luckily they didn't. Phew!

15. Acle Regatta

~ *Boswell's Broadland*

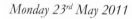

Monday 23rd May 2011

16. Langley Dyke looking towards Cantley
Oil on board 14" x 12"

Location; Halfway along Langley Dyke on the west bank
Weather; Brilliant sunshine with very strong westerly wind.

I took the wheelbarrow today but there was really no need as I was able to capture the essence of the scene and incorporate the Cantley sugar beet silos in the distance. For sailors on this stretch of the Yare, they form a windbreak when yachts are trying to get down to Reedham and beyond. I spoke to just one man as he concentrated his attention on a group of heifers and a bull being herded into a field. The man had his cruiser in the dyke and was loathe to move as his wife was not confident in mooring up in a strong wind.

I am getting to rather like the area with its amazing sweep of marshes and cattle. I made a small detour to Hardley Staithe but will forego painting there as it will be much the same as this painting. Perhaps a little picture of The Chet might be quite nice or Loddon, neither of which I am familiar with.

H. Percival

16. Langley Dyke, looking towards Cantley

~ *Boswell's Broadland*

17. Loddon Staithe

Oil on board 15" x 12"

Location; By the car park at Loddon Staithe looking towards the boat yards.

Weather; A dull day with just a slight breeze from the northwest. Occasional showers.

I made an early start today as the forecast was not looking good but as with sods law it all came good as I was leaving. It's quite a nice spot being so close to the heart of the village. On the left is a modern development by Roy Williamson Properties with their own private moorings. Christine, of 'her indoors' fame, designed and installed several of the private gardens there. The site, now fully occupied, looks like it has matured well. To the right are the public moorings and distant views of two boatyards.

Being a fairly public place I had my photograph taken by a nice couple, Mr and Mrs Barry Head, originally from Swaffham but visiting for a fortnights boating holiday. They said that the weather had been good but had struggled with the wind when mooring up. A local businessman admired my painting and told me he was a diver doing work all over the world. I didn't have the cheek to ask him to retrieve my oil paints near the Carrow Bridge in Norwich.

It was a lovely subject to paint, if interrupted but the odd shower. On completion I returned a coffee cup I had from Rosie Lee's Tea Rooms opposite and popped into Loddon Mills Art building run by Andrew and Katherine Walker. A grant aided venue which has everything from visiting jazz musicians, comedy club, classic evenings and much more. They have also started to have art exhibitions from time to time so might consider this at a later date.

The mill was originally owned by Woods, Sadd and Moore who had hired Irish navvies to dig out the staithe to take a fleet of wherries that they owned moving milled products, seed and coal up and down the Yare between Norwich and Yarmouth.

Time for home to get ready for Thurne Regatta starting tomorrow. The weather forecast sounds grim. Hey ho.

17. Loddon Staithe

~ *Boswell's Broadland*

18. Thurne Regatta

Oil on board 16" x 11"

Location; Adjacent to moored river boats upstream from the regatta tent

Weather; Strong winds dominated with grey skies. Wind had dropped by mid afternoon

Thurne lived up to its reputation with challenging sailing. Two reefs being the order of the day and intermittent drizzly showers.

My only solution for painting was to find a semi sheltered spot in the lee of some alders and hope for the best. With my box easel firmly weighted down I set to my task. For the most part it was quite a dull light, brightened only by the colourful striped awning of the regatta tent. This is a long way from boyhood memories when the tent was an ex-army one in camouflage prone to take charge when high winds were evident. It was extremely heavy and required an army of enthusiastic East Anglian Cruising Club members to put it up. A proper metal bridge and adjacent parking are now welcome additions not to mention serried ranks of portaloos. Formerly there was a canvas awning for the men with 360 degree views. The latrine with Elsan toilet was something else. One year it toppled down the bank with 'Big John' still inside. He was not welcome in the bar afterwards. For the most part things stay the same with the Thurne Mills still dominating the landscape and the little green bungalow close by . Parties there during the regatta were legendary with the old members of the so called 'Ranworth Yacht Squadron' heavily in attendance. Frank Potter and Pat Larner are very much fondly remembered.

The regatta is dominated for the most part by the Cruiser Class and today, even heavily reefed, some still sported topsails. The colourful sails of Beth and *Blue Jacket,* I have tried to fit into my painting. The boats, during racing, stretch as far as the eye can see from my viewpoint. Downstream towards Acle and upstream to St Benets Abbey. Quite a fantastic sight.

There was a continuous stream of people passing my painting position and it was good to get a wave from Mike Barnes and family, greetings from Patrick Richardson and Jeremy Tusting. There was a charming group of children who complimented me on my painting, all kitted out in the obligatory life jackets. They reminded me so much of my own two girls, Natalie and Sophie, when they were little. They would roam along the riverbank getting on and off friends' boats. At one Thurne Regatta Sophie pitched head first through the open hatch of our sailing cruiser and we ended up in the Norfolk and Norwich hospital for an overnight check for concussion. That was the end of our regatta for that weekend. My painting, I hope, did some justice to the scene and perhaps over the next two days I will return to do some drawing.

Smuggler sailing Cruiser No.145 when she was in Herbert Woods hire fleet

18. Thurne Regatta

~ *Boswell's Broadland*

19. Reedham Ferry Inn and crossing

Oil on board 14" x 12"

Location; On the quay heading 150 yards from the Inn and ferry boat

Weather; Bright and sunny with a slight breeze. Showers forecast later which didn't materialise

I approached the ferry crossing point by taking the Hales turn off and left again. The road leads through lovely countryside near to the Ravingham Estate and comes close by the river for some way with an old mill now occupied as a house.

Bob the ferryman was kind enough to allow me to go back and forth to 'recci' a good painting spot which turned out to be the other side of the river. There were one or two foot passengers and a small boy shook the hands of the ferryman in thanks. What politeness. Later on, whilst painting, a party of children being transported had their helium filled balloons out of the windows of a four by four. It looked like the ferry had Christmas decorations. I believe, years ago coming this way, the ferry would carry a decorated Christmas tree on board. Perhaps they still do.

The Inn these days is run by David Archer building on the business his father, Norman, started in 1949. My father knew his dad quite well and he must be congratulated on taking it on originally as it was in a parlous state just after the war. The ferry wasn't working and there was little money after the war for materials. The Inn now thrives and the ferry has had several refits since those early days.

I once painted David in a picture, unbeknown to him, when commissioned to cover a shoot at Strumpsham Hall for Jimmy Key. David, if I remember is a left handed shot. Inside the pub is really old and I took a good look at old photos of previous landlords and wherrymen. In one modern photo I spotted Kurt Angelrath, someone I knew, beaming away. Still looking good Kurt.

Back over the ferry to show Bob my painting and gave him one of my cards as he was interested in my previous books.

John Ellis on *Bluejacket*

19. Reedham Ferry Inn and Crossing

~ *Boswell's Broadland*

20. Reedham with Swing Bridge

Oil on board 11.5" x 9"

Location; 200 yards upstream from the swing bridge

Weather; Another virtually cloudless sunny day with a light South-Westerly breeze.

As an old sailing cruiser man the thought of sailing through the bridge makes me feel particularly nervous. On approaching it in the open position it is liable to shut with an imminent train coming with very little notice. Today felt very much the same as I started painting the bridge which was fully closed, facing the sun. Within no time it had opened. I then spent most of the morning painting an incongruously shut bridge. An artist's sod's law. Having said all that this is a great place to paint the bridge as it is quite picturesque with Sanderson Craft Marine boatsheds at one end of the village, the Lord Nelson PH in the centre and the bridge and Ship Inn PH at the other end.

For a change, because of where I was standing, a few people came and spoke to me. The quayside Broads Authority man told me about the bridge being over 100 years old and that the chain mechanism is so quiet that even after all these years it is difficult to hear it when in operation.

Later that day I climbed above the village looking down on the bridge with the beautiful marshes spread out all around. The new cut starts just around the corner going off into the distance in a straight line. Go straight ahead for Oulton Broad or follow the river to the left for Breydon Water. A few holidaymakers spoke to me together with a professional artist who liked my painting.

By lunchtime I was hungry and tried the aptly named 'Cup cakes Coffee and Tea Rooms' run by Annette and Robert Terry for paninis and coffee. Home shortly thereafter.

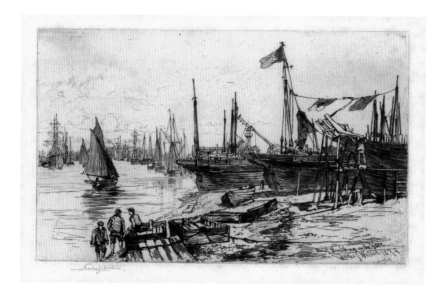

C. J. Watson 1879
BOAT BUILDING ON THE YARE

20. Reedham and Reedham Swing Bridge

~ *Boswell's Broadland*

21. St. Olaves Bridge

Oil on board 14" x 12"

Location; 150 metres from St. Olaves bridge opposite South River Marine

Weather; Cloudy start with sunshine by mid morning. A steady southerly breeze.

I took the footpath along the river bank which was just wide enough to take my easel. Luckily only a couple and two young lads with bikes came past all morning and were quite happy to climb over the sea defence wall. My choice of painting this side of the bridge was so I was able to paint South River marine with large sea going yachts moored up together with the yards ' crane. The morning soon passed and although I had to alter the tone of my painting as the day brightened it was not too much of a problem.

Thirsty work this painting so called into The Bell Inn opposite. Very low ceilings and quite nice. The Inn is reputed to be the oldest recorded in Broadland, built on the site of a former ferry crossing where the ferryman's wages were in bread and fish. Close by is the remains of an Augustine Priory which were often built at these crossing points.

I didn't call in to see Steve Smith at South River as they seemed to be busy launching a river cruiser. St Olaves is particularly attractive as you approach it over the Haddiscoe Bridge which crosses the New Cut. This gives great views across Chedgrave and Thurlton marshes. A friend, Rachael Hipperson who is a land manager of this area said she could get me access to these marshes which stretch from Breydon Water to the New Cut in a large triangle of land. We shall have to see if there is time.

21. St Olave's Bridge

~ Boswell's Broadland

The Three Rivers Race

I set off late from my home and parked on the Horning to Ludham road. It was quite staggering the amount of people who had come to watch the race and was testament to the ever increasing popularity of this event. I have competed myself helming a white boat Oak Beauty with Liz Bryan and sundry crewing jobs with Patrick Richardson's *Slipstream* where we acquitted ourselves well.

For those who are not familiar with the format of this race, boats set off in their class categories at set times from Horning sailing club and have to navigate around the buoys located inside South Walsham Broad, below Ludham Bridge, Hickling Broad and a buoy downstream of Acle Bridge; in their chosen order. In other words, navigating the Bure, Ant and Thurne rivers, hence the races' name. Prizes are awarded for each category of boat together with the fastest time sailed for the overall winner.

Competitors set off this Saturday in a fresh-ish North-Easterly wind which would have allowed long periods of reaching for a major part of the course. The Ant section, however, would have necessitated some tight tacking. The skill of the race is, of course, taking the right decisions with the lower Bure buoy being the one that catches most people out. This is the tidal section of the course. If night falls together with the wind many an unhappy sailor will have to navigate waiting 'til tides turn or winds increase. The forecast for this particular race had fresh winds throughout the night so there should be some early arrivals after midnight from the early starters between 11.00 and 12.00 in the morning.

I spoke to Liz and Bernard Bryan together with Hugh Ferrier on the very crowded Swan lawn as we watched the various fleets depart. Liz's sons Giles and Simon were competing with their own cruisers. It was a fantastic sight as they sped off down Horning Street. I know from experience that there will be some tired little boys and girls in the early hours of the morning tomorrow. Good luck to them.

P.S. Mike Barnes should receive a putty medal for excellent reverse procedure in *Wyoma* across the whole width of the river without slamming into The Swan quay heading.

23. Somerleyton Swing Bridge

Oil on board 10" x 8"

Location; On the small car park upstream from the bridge. The Duke's Head PH close by

Weather; Patchy rain with occasional heavy rain downpour. Wind light North-Westerly

I knew what the day would be like having seen the TV weather forecast depicting rain most of the morning but brightening up later.

Arriving a little bit early at Somerleyton I popped into the post office, an award winning village store, for a coffee. Sold a couple of books and chatted to the owner about her time spent in Africa and subsequently in France. A lovely little place with resident parrot in the corner to keep customers entertained. On leaving, the weather was still bad so I called into the Estate Office at Somerleyton Hall to see if they would stock my book *Boswell's Coast*. It's good enough for the National Trust at Blickling so hopefully the same will apply here.

The little staithe that I painted from gave a good view of the bridge, unfortunately in the closed position this time. I was hoping it would be open for a change. Sods law I suppose. Not much traffic on the river apart from the odd private cruiser coming out of moorings close to the bridge. I spotted a boat called *Thumper,* at one time owned by Raymond Jeckells of sail and chandlery family business. Perhaps he was helming. A few holidaymakers from adjacent moored boats came to say 'hello' on their way to the shops and The Dukes Head. I called in there on the way home for a drink and sampled their chicken tikka skewer, pitta bread and coleslaw. Delicious. The menu consists of fresh local produce, sourced from the Somerleyton estate, including beef; Lowestoft for fresh fish and Suffolk for their local pork. A visit to the Slugs Lane pub is well worth a trip.

P.S. Somerleyton is the birthplace of the hovercraft

PPS. Musac playing 'Sha la la Pretty Flamingo' could have had me doing a Dad's dance to all concerned. Not a pretty sight.

23. Somerleyton Swing Bridge

~ *Boswell's Broadland*

24. Oulton Broad and Wherry Hotel

Oil on board 15" x 12"
Location; On the yacht station side next to Nicholas Everett Park.

Weather; Sunny but with changeable and cloudy conditions. Winds moderate but decreasing

The Harbour Master, Jerry Hilder, one of the team, gave me permission to paint just the other side of a barrier with access to private motor vessels. It was a bit like having my own compound surrounded on three sides by rails. The weather was so changeable with a fairly strong breeze so I set to my task with endeavour. In the distance stood the Wherry Hotel standing majestically at the end of the Broad and to my left are the large Truman buildings formerly maltings but now converted to flats.

It was many years ago that I worked for Lancer Marine on that side of the broad, as a GRP laminator. Well paid but pretty sticky work. Oulton Broad is best known for its regatta but more of that later. The Mutford Lock is beautifully restored and gives access to Lake Lothian and the North Sea. This area was a hive of activity during the war with the building of wooden naval vessels servicing the fleet and patrolling our coast either as attack vessels or rescue for RAF personnel downed at sea. Brook Marine was one of many yards doing this work as well as H.T. Percival of Horning and Herbert Woods of Potter Heigham amongst others.

The Oulton Yacht Station reminded me of my youth when Bill Solomon administered the moorings. My father's boat *Sea Girl* and later *Rombo* regularly moored here before passing through the lock en route for the RNSYC yacht basin. Happy Days.

I spoke to quite a few people today and one man was on his fifth holiday on the Broads and is a testament to its' enduring appeal. I had a quick coffee at the quayside cafe and wandered over to admire the *Southern Belle*. She was built in 1925 in Plymouth, now owned by Steve Wilson who also runs Waveney River Tours with The *Waveney Princess,* another fine craft, built in the sixties. No time for much else but had a drink in The Lady of The Lake PH and wandered into Jeckells Chandlery next door looking for shackles. P.S An old boy stopped me in the street and said they were offering a two course lunch at The Lady of the Lake for £4.50. I must look like a starving artist and hard- up to boot.

24. Oulton Broad and Wherry Hotel
~ Boswell's Broadland

25. The Royal Norfolk and Suffolk Yacht Club and Basin

Oil on board 15" x 12"
Location; Above the gangway for the lifeboat looking towards the yacht club and basin
Weather; A warm but cloudy day with a light south westerly breeze

I am mindful of the fact that this yacht club has royal patronage with the present patron being the Duke of Edinburgh. It is an architectural masterpiece designed by George Skipper of Norwich. Other buildings to his credit are The Royal Arcade and the Norwich Union Headquarters. It was built in the Arts and Crafts style and has walls that splay outwards like buttresses and is peppered with round windows, perhaps mimicking the portholes of boats. The club has recently celebrated its one hundred and fiftieth anniversary.

You may wonder why a Lowestoft yacht club would be included in my series of paintings of the Broads. The answer is simply that the Broads sailors, since Victorian times, have competed in races and regattas both offshore here at Lowestoft and throughout Broadland. Yachts had professional skippers then but with the advent of boats being built to a one- design things have changed. The club attracts a large number of Brown boats for its Sea Week regatta, together with races for yachtsmen throughout the summer months.

I have a slight connection with the club as my father was a member together with his friend Percival of Horning, who both kept their motor vessels here. I made many a scary passage to Belgium and Holland with them navigating by dead reckoning at night time. My job was to go up on deck to get a weather forecast from my transistor radio. None of this high tech stuff then.

Incidentally, my father's cousin, Dr. David Boswell of Oulton Broad, was Rear Commodore of the club in the mid-fifties. He owned the first Brown boat, No. 1, called *Dunlin*, built in 1900 and sailed it with his daughter Sarah.

It's always a delight to be by the coast and I spoke at length to various holidaymakers, Mr and Mrs Boakes. They liked the picture and will look out for my books in Waterstones.

My time was soon up but it was a pleasure to paint such a lovely scene. Edward Seago painted a lovely view of moored yachts from the clubhouse and used a little artistic license I gather. He was eventually made an honorary member of the club.

Home by Somerleyton Hall, St. Olaves and eventually Haddiscoe Hall to pick up paintings from a previous exhibition staged by Rosemary de Vere. I don't suppose I shall get much more painting done this week with a poor weather forecast and sadly a memorial service for artist David Potter to be held at Potter on Friday. He will be sadly missed from the local art scene.

25. The Royal Norfolk and Suffolk Yacht Club and basin

~ *Boswell's Broadland*

26. Beccles River View

Oil on board 15" x 12"

Location;Opposite the WaveneyHotel 200yards downstream

Weather; Sunny day with no breeze. Outlook for the afternoon – rainy.

My original intention was to paint the river with Beccles magnificent church in the background. As it turned out I chose to face the other way and painted an old converted granary or maltings, owned I believe by Dr. Jan de Vere. Beccles on the far bank has lovely houses leading down to the river with their own private moorings and boat houses. There was very little boat activity so the reflections of buildings and trees proved pretty attractive. Over on my side of the river only a few passers-by stopped to say 'Hi' and 'what a lovely spot this is'. Walkers could follow the bank to the Geldeston Locks Inn and catch the Big Dog Ferry if they timed it right.

A quick call later to the centre of this lovely town where I met Lee Mason who agreed to stock *Boswell's Coast* at his new shop, Beccles Books. Good luck to him.

PS. I talked to a gentleman cutting the grass by the river moorings who said he received free moorings for his boat at Oulton in return for this service. When I cut the grass at home I get given another task!

C. M. Wigg
BECCLES

26. Beccles river view

~ *Boswell's Broadland*

Friday 24th June 2011

27. The Locks Inn, Geldeston

Oil on board 10" x 8"

Location; The Geldeston Locks pub in the middle of the Beccles marshes

Weather; The forecast was sunny early on with rain coming in from the west later.

I left quite early this morning because I was uncertain that the river ferry, *Big Dog*, would be running at the right time for me. I did a recce to Geldeston village to see how close I could get to the pub. It turns out that a fairly decent unmade-up track takes you right up to the pub. The last time that I was here was over twenty years ago and I arrived in a group of sailing cruisers so I was surprised to see the place as it is now. The little pub which had no electricity and no proper bar has been extended to two large side wings although the original central building is still in place.

Back in the times of the old wherries this was a busy stopping off point for a thirsty wherryman before passing through the locks on the way to Bungay. Alas the lock has fallen into disrepair in the sixties and navigation stops here.

I crossed over a small dyke accessed by a new bridge and spoke at length to a local man with his dog who took upon himself to pick up litter and bottles from this idyllic spot. My painting took in a distant view of the Locks Inn resting amongst the trees and reflecting in the river before me. Early morning with few people or boats about, I was able to take in the beautiful marshlands in peace. Distant groups of cattle grazed contentedly with the river itself the centre of attention for bird life turning on the wing over the water.

Home via Bungay to pick up some of my paintings from The Cork Brick Gallery. Ken Skipper was not there but his wife helped me load my car.

27. The Locks Inn, Geldeston

~ *Boswell's Broadland*

28. The Berney Arms Mill and pub.

Oil on board 11.5" x 9"

Location; Two hundred yards upstream from the mill on the high river bank. Looking towards the old pub and the entrance to Breydon Water.

Weather; The hottest day of the year by far. Temperatures in the low thirties but were tempered by a strong warm breeze from the south from Spain apparently.

There are only two ways to reach this spot, reputedly Britain's most isolated pub, by boat and train. The train did it for me as I hadn't taken these marshland trains before or even stopped at Berney. My companion on this trip was my friend Paul Darley, a well-known Cromer artist who knew this area well. As a seasoned public transport traveller I bowed to his superior knowledge as he is able to navigate through the British Rail timetable. For my part I boarded the 11.36am to Berney. The train makes only one stop here so Paul told the guard to tell the driver to make a stop. On our return there is just the one train at 3.30pm to bring us home so it made for an anxious painting time. Paul remembers in the past frantically waving to the driver to stop who only just spotted him and stopped some way down the track. On another time he had his bike and, missing the train, had to navigate miles of marshes and locked farm gates to reach the main road.

Paul Darley painting at Berney Arms

The journey from Norwich took only half an hour and it was quite nice to see places I had painted in the past few months from the comfort of my seat. 'The Reedcutters' at Thorpe Green, Postwick Grove, Langley and Hardley, all whizzed past. On disembarking, luckily it was only a short walk with our gear to the river bank. With the benefit of hindsight the best view would have been the mill with old farm houses in the background but I needed to feature the pub as well. Conditions were difficult to paint with the sun and wind on our backs. Paul's easel blew over in the wind but thankfully no damage was done.

By lunchtime I needed to shelter from the heat and I left Paul to finish his painting while I went to the pub. The mill and pub are inextricably linked with the former originally used for crushing chalk and clay to make cement. Clay from Breydon and chalk from pits at Whitlingham transported by the old wherries of the day, thus providing good trade for the pub today run by Tracey Bold and John Ralph.

Two very weary painters made their way back to the railway stop and reflected on this beautiful and isolated stop. Luscious grassland with grazing cattle reminded me of the enduring paintings by Arnesby Brown who made the subject virtually his own in this part of the world. It still exists today for all to appreciate in its natural form. My ancestors, incidentally, were cattle drovers from Forfar in Fife and brought cattle to these very same grazing marshes in the seventeenth and eighteenth century to be fattened up for market in Norwich.

28. Berney Arms Mill and PH

~ *Boswell's Broadland*

C. J. Watson, 1918
NORFOLK MARSHES

29. Breydon Water

Oil on board 20" x 10"

Location ; On the edge of Breydon Water by the Wherryman's Way footpath, adjacent to Asda car park.

Weather; Sunny with a slight northerly breeze

I took the footpath from Asda car park by Yarmouth railway station, passing under Breydon Bridge. Although quite a low position by the water's edge it did still facilitate a fabulous view with the bridge to my left sweeping around into the distance with Berney Mill slightly visible on the horizon. Around to my right was a glimpse of the Acle Straight. In this direction along the footpath was an elevated bird watching hut which I thought might be suitable as a painting position. It was quite cold and dark in there and was occupied by bird watchers; Keith, Bob and Tony who told me where there were good spots if I wanted to do further Breydon paintings.

The water was at high tide so could only see a few wading birds mixed in with gulls on the waters' edge.

With direct sunlight from behind me it offered not the best painting conditions but I was able to complete my work within a relatively short time. There were a few craft making their way up Breydon towards Oulton and Norwich which was a surprise as it didn't appear to be slack water. Perhaps there was too much water coming through the yacht station from the River Bure. Low water would be a better option later on.

With the ever changing clouds passing overhead it made for some dramatic light playing on the water. I hope my picture captured some elements of this.

29. Breydon Water

~ *Boswell's Broads*

30. Yarmouth Yacht station and North-West tower.

Oil on board 14" x 12"

Location; On the boundary of the yacht station looking downstream towards the old north west tower with road and old discontinued railway bridge distant.

Weather; What can I say but sunny again with a very light breeze.

Generally speaking this is not my favourite place in the world. I think it is past experience of arriving too early on the tide and trying to moor up. Once I was in an old converted lifeboat and a passing holiday-maker's boat had broken down and was out of control being swept away under the strong tide. I shouted for him to throw his mooring line to me, which he did but he had failed to remove a lethal rond anchor still attached, nearly hitting me on the head. Panic over.

Another journey in very windy conditions, necessitated a whole flotilla of yachts to moor up on land upstream from the yacht station. A man came flying out and said "You can't moor here, it's private" to which Patrick Richardson told him in no uncertain terms "That's what you think, don't you know who I am?". This shut him up and he sloped off leaving us to wait for the tide and conditions to improve.

The Broads Authority's harbour master couldn't have been more helpful and went out of his way in allowing me to park and set up my easel with a good view point. The station land runs for several hundred metres with road and pavement running parallel so I had a constant stream of people passing comments. One family were from Glasgow who were having a great holiday and we spoke briefly about the Glasgow School of Art. He was wearing a Rangers tee shirt and I thought it prudent not to talk about football, not that I am a Celtic supporter.

Well there you have the starting point of my journey to the northern rivers and Broads with the Bure beckoning me. Let's hope wind, weather and tide remain favourable.

C. J. Watson
LOW TIDE YARMOUTH, May 1894

30. Yarmouth Yacht Station and North-West Tower

~ *Boswell's Broadland*

31. Stracey Windpump, Acle New Road.

Oil on board 14" x 12"

Location; Downstream from the Stracey Mill buildings on the high river bank

Weather; Warm with scuddingclouds

I made an early start today and was painting by 8.30am. My daughter Sophie and fiancée Ryan were heading back to Norfolk from their Inn, *The Shears* in Wiltshire, so wanted to get as much done as possible. Many years ago I painted this same scene but stood on the side of the road which, on reflection, was a very dangerous thing to do considering the volume of traffic.

There was quite a collection of boats moored up all calling in to the shop and tea rooms run by owners Tony and Sue Brightwell. Tony said he had been here 21 years and had created quite a nice little business. They kept animals that ran free along the bank, goats, ponies and donkeys, all who were quite tame. The holidaymakers love them and can visit the mill for a small fee as well. I spoke to quite a few including one man who was with his son's stag party. He looked a bit bleary-eyed. They started their journey at Burgh Castle but had ended up by taxi in Yarmouth. They were having a good old fry-up in the tea rooms before heading off to Stalham for a lunch time carvery. I asked him if he wouldn't be late for work on Monday? He said "No matter, I am the boss".

In contrast to The Berny Arms mill The Stracey Mill was more picturesque insofar as the sail battens on one arm were missing giving it more gravitas with a single spa set against the sky line.

Home by lunchtime after negotiating a very dangerous reverse procedure onto the Acle Straight. *Phew.*

C. M. Wigg
A NORFOLK WINDMILL

31. Stracey Wind Pump, Acle New Road

~ *Boswell's Broadland*

32. Stokesby Staithe

Oil on board 14" x 12"

Location; Upstream from the Ferry Inn at Stokesby by the village green.

Weather; A bright start with thundery clouds building up .A slight breeze.

I was glad to be on the road again so to speak after a few days in Portugal to recharge the batteries. I drove to Stokesby village for the first time which is quite attractive. The Ferry Inn dominates the river frontage with moorings on the bend in the river for several hundred yards each side. There were only a few boats moored up when I arrived at breakfast time and I was kindly offered a coffee by Mark Lacey, a boating holidaymaker from Derby. He was on his own as his wife had gone to stay with relatives as she felt unwell. We spoke at length about his job as a heating and air conditioning engineer and the problems with working on Listed Buildings.

A family group from Wiltshire moored up obstructing my view but I continued painting like a true professional.

The Inn itself sits nicely on the waterfront surrounded by picturesque cottages. Wherries and lighters would have made this a busy place in Victorian times especially as this was one of the old ferry points across the Bure.

With the sun in my eyes and the ever changing clouds I struggled to keep the tone of my work together. However, in due course I finished and made my way to the local store visiting an artist's studio along the way. Russell Canham had recently given up architectural work to concentrate on his art. Best of luck old boy. His studio was quite charming and faced his Georgian house across well kept gardens. I am glad that I made the effort to go to Stokesby as I originally had intended to miss it and go to Acle as my next port of call.

C. M. Wigg
STOKESBY

32. Stokesby Staithe

~ *Boswell's Broadland*

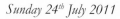

33. Acle Bridge Inn

Oil on board

Location; Downstream from Acle Bridge with the pub and gardens adjacent.

Weather; Very blustery, windy conditions but quite warm and sunny. North west wind direction.

Unlike me, I decided to work on a Sunday and I am glad that I made the effort. A bit cold to start with but the sunny conditions made the river sparkle and added extra emphasis to my picture. Various holidaymakers spoke to me admiring my painting including a man moored under the bridge with a rising tide. The boat looked as if it was on the point of floating onto the low quay heading at this point. Tragically, a man drowned falling from a cruiser at this very place last week. At any rate the holidaymakers were having fun with children playing in the pub gardens with attendant dads. One even wanted to buy my painting when it is next exhibited.

On the way home I called into the Norfolk Broads Yacht Club to get permission to paint there next week as it is the start of their annual regatta. Looks like it is going to be a belter. Spoke briefly to Geoff Coulthard, Sue Platt as was and Mike Batson as is. Lets hope the weather holds for all of them.

C. M. Wigg
NORFOLK WHERRIES

33. Acle Bridge Inn

~ *Boswell's Broadland*

34. Wroxham Regatta

Oil on board 14" x 12"

Location; Adjacent to the Club Steward's office with overview of clubhouse and broad.

Weather; Cloudy and overcast with a light westerly wind.

It was really great to return to the Norfolk Broads Yacht Club and members were most welcoming but I think slightly bemused having an artist planted down amongst them. Because the regatta races change regularly on the hour, technically my picture was most challenging. I started with the Broads One Design race and finished with the lunchtime River Cruisers racing. I wanted to depict the essence of Wroxham Regatta so concentrated on the clubhouse with its' figures and let the boats racing take up the background.

All went well until I failed to remember the colours of the Broads One Design class flag. Luckily I mentioned this to a man from the Norfolk Wherry Trust who proceeded to take off his belt which was coloured with all the class flags. Trousers managed to stay up despite this. My flag showed the race with less than five minutes to the start but in reality it took me some time to paint the boats in after the race had commenced. Hey ho.

There was a steady stream of people that I knew from my past association with the club. Peter Jeckells spoke about Robert Dawson-Smith and The Saracen's Head. Glynn Howarth kindly offered me his reedlighter boat to paint from. Incidentally he had spotted me painting at Stokesby a few days ago. Ken Lord and his wife stopped for a chat. Willie Bentall with the illustrious *Forester* offered encouragement. Robin Richardson, Alan Mallet, Hugh Ferrier,and John Atkins all spoke to me briefly and caught up with old times.

Many happy memories of times racing here in my youth and indeed of thirteen years attending with my fine River Cruiser *Smuggler* No. 145. My, how things have changed with inboard engines for the river cruisers and no one quanting off the quay heading. No bad thing. Perhaps the greatest change for the club is the building of the lagoon. I suppose you can call it progress as in my day it was no more than a mosquito-infested area. Now beautifully landscaped and peopled with very large motor cruisers. Good for income and good for the increased vitality of the club.

Tired but pleased with my day I hope to return another time if at all possible.

34. Wroxham Regatta

~ *Boswell's Broadland*

35. Upton Dyke and Eastwood Whelpton's Yard.

Oil on board 14" x 12"

Location; At the end of Upton Dyke adjacent to Eastwood Whelpton's boatyard.

Weather; Warm but cloudy with a light northerly wind

I spoke briefly to Anne Whelpton at her yard before starting painting. Tim Whelpton, her late husband, was well known in yachting circles not only as an Olympic sailor with the Star class but with Timothy Colman and others built and challenged the world sailing speed record with their boats *Crossbow 1* and *2* gaining a new world record with both boats.

It was quite a sunny spot to paint with a steady stream of holidaymakers heading for the dustbins next to me. Some might say the bins are a good spot for my work, however a local artist, Colin Giles, came to say hello which was nice. Dog walkers proliferated together with hikers heading off on a circular route which starts from this point. As the day brightened I looked with envy at those on the water. The last time I was here was to launch my boat *Wings* to attend Acle Regatta as I couldn't launch at Acle without a public slipway there. Home via South Walsham.

The Smuggler Launching Party, Potter Heigham 1906

35. Upton Dyke

~ *Boswell's Broadland*

Thurne mill,
Norfolk.

H.J. Starling
THURNE MILL

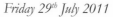
36. Thurne Dyke

Oil on board 15" x 12"

Location; At one end of Thurne Dyke opposite the Red Lion pub.

Weather; Overcast and on the cold side. Light wind from the north east

I arrived early at Thurne which was a bit of a mistake because it was cold and dreary. By the time it had brightened up I was on the way home. I was surprised how busy the village was with cyclists, camp site and boat people all milling around. Many spoke to me and talked about their holidays. A large group had come out from Norwich to camp. Kids, dogs and all. They were having a wonderful time. It's an old truism that beauty and the good life are often found on your door step.

Thurne is well known to me as I often stayed and visited my friends John and Sheila Lawrence at Oby Rectory which is just up the road. Thurne Regatta was well indulged by us all on many occasions. In my youth drinks at *The Red Lion* run by Reg and Thelma Parsons was a precursor to racing out at Thurne Mouth. Thurne is dominated by its two windmills, one on the opposite bank slightly downstream from the dyke, with the white tower of Thurne mill dominating the end of the dyke. Edward Seago, I believe, painted the dyke from the other end to me and his small charming picture hangs in the Castle Museum, Norwich. It consists mainly of sailing boats moored up. Nowadays the scene is dominated by motor cruisers.

I returned home to Wymondham via Ludham and Wroxham which were very congested with the holiday traffic. My next port of call could be Womack Water approaching, I think this time, via the Norwich Southern bypass.

36. Thurne Dyke

~ *Boswell's Broadland*

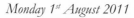

37. Beccles Regatta

Oil on board 15" x 12"

Location; Adjacent to the starting box at Beccles Amateur Sailing Club.

Weather; Sunny with a temperature of about 20 degrees. A moderate South-Easterly wind was blowing.

There is something a bit special for me about Beccles Regatta. I suppose first and foremost it's the location on a bend in the river with Beccles and its church on the horizon. I sailed here quite a lot as a boy and it was lovely to see such a mixed range of craft participating. Lasers, Toppers, Waveneys, Norfolks and quite a strong fleet of Enterprise dinghys.

Ray Johnson crewed by Wendy Bush, and also Geoff Coulthard were participating and I spoke to them briefly. It really was busy here on the bank with people to-ing and fro-ing all the time admiring my progress. One couple said they would come back in a couple of hours when I had finished, only to be told that the picture was all but done! David Talks, a watercolour artist from Norwich spoke to me about his exhibition. Quite a nice impressionist artist after my own heart.

The tone of my painting was quite subdued so gave my picture a slightly different look. I hope it worked. Next port of call will be Horning Sailing Club's Regatta so will have to work quite hard this month as the regatta season is well under way.

My wife, Christine at the helm of my sailing boat, *Wings*

37. Beccles Regatta

~ *Boswell's Broadland*

38. Horning Regatta

Oil on board 16" x 11"

Location; On the green facing the river with Horning Sailing Club to the right hand side.

Weather; A sunny day with a light south westerly.

Horning Regatta, for me, was the start of my racing and sailing experience. Aged about 11 or 12 I sailed against the likes of Mike Evans, Enterprise and National champion and Tom Percival, National and future Power Boat champion. Other club members at the time were George Southgate, David Hastings, John Pacey, Tony Knights, John Withers and many other names lost in the sands of time. I could see today the ethos of the club hasn't changed and is still a very friendly place. Lots of young sailors in Toppers and Lasers for the main part, made for a colourful fleet.

I spoke to no end of club members, in particular a lady owner of Rebel no 10, who I believe went on to win the morning race. Mike Batson told me his first cousin is Graham Howlett, a fellow artist. A fact after all these years I didn't know. The owners of The *Southern Comfort* passenger ferry were kind enough to let me know they were going out at 10.30am to return at 12.00 noon, if I wanted to finish their boat in my picture. How kind.

My father kept his wherry houseboat *Arcadia* in the lagoon by the Petersfield Hotel along The Street. Every Saturday morning I would tow my Enterprise *Zuleika* with our launch, along The Street to the clubhouse. On one occasion my father crewed me and we ended up in the drink. Last time I called upon his services! My sister Anne helmed one race and managed to hole Tim Whelpton's *Star* which he wasn't well pleased about. Glad I was just crewing at the time.

Happy days at Horning especially regatta week culminating at a dance at the village hall close by. Latter years saw me switch my allegiance to Wroxham Sailing Club but I always remember my time at Horning with fond memories.

John Dudley Boswell, my father

38. Horning Regatta

~ *Boswell's Broadland*

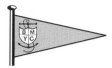

H.J. Starling
POTTER HEIGHAM BRIDGE. 1889

Patrick Richardson
of Phoenix Fleet
Boatyards

39. Potter Heigham

Oil on board 15" x 12"

Location; Next to Phoenix Fleet's offices for their launches and river pilot service.

Weather; Sunny with broken clouds later, a light breeze.

Potter or Potter 'Hedron' affectionately called by locals, was pretty busy. Patrick and Robin Richardson, owners of the boatyard, greeted me and we chatted about the previous Wroxham Regatta and forthcoming Sea Week at Lowestoft. Patrick was clearing out his late father's house and had a magnificent model of *Excelsior* his father had made. Sadly, another of the old model steamers that he was making, was only half-finished. Let's hope they find good homes.

I was quite surprised how busy this spot I had chosen was with customers arriving to hire the little electric launches, Phoenix being one of the pioneering yards to start them on the Broads. My old yacht *Smuggler* often over-wintered here and classic boats are still being restored here today with a Yare and Bure One Design being renovated together with another classic river cruiser.

Lots of holidaymakers admired the finished painting and Patrick was pleased I had made an effort and placed his collie dog in the picture. I said I would mention Patrick in my next book. "Don't worry" he said " I'm famous enough already". I asked his postman who was calling at the yard jokingly if there were any letters for me and he said he didn't deliver to travelling artists.

39. Potter Heigham Bridge

~ *Boswell's Broadland*

Sunday 7th August 2011

40. Sea Week, Lowestoft

Oil on board 16" x 11

Location; Painted close by the South Pier pavilion on the beach

Weather; Sunny day with a fresh South-Westerly wind

Arrived in Lowestoft a little bit early for the racing, with the Broads One Designs starting at 10.50am. I did a quick sortie to the clubhouse just to see boat preparations. I wanted to know whether the boats would head off in the Pakefield direction where my easel was set up on the beach. A kind lady who wasn't sailing said a decision would be made by the officer of the day when the boats came out to sea.

It was a bit like waiting for greyhounds to exit the trap, waiting on the beach for the boats so I busied myself painting ancillary areas of my canvas to get things in scale. As it turned out the BODs came out in a fairly steady straggle and I managed to get a few on to canvas. The sea conditions were just lovely with the sun sparkling on the water and casting those lovely shadows so reminiscent of many a Norwich School painting and latterly works such as Campbell Mellon and Rowland Fisher making this part of the coastline their own.

The process of painting outdoors can be tricky with the well meaning holidaymakers talking to you and passing comments. I thought I had cracked it this time by painting very close to the sea wall. The public are a canny lot and managed to talk to me none the less on top of the wall. One nice local photographer took my photo and said he would send it to the EDP. He didn't give his name but let's hope the editor is in a good mood tomorrow.

There was a charity fete taking place on the green close by for the local hospital fund, accompanied by the Endeavour Rangers band. I asked one young man what the name of the band was. He didn't know. Good job he wasn't the conductor, bless him.

Fond memories of sailing in my Enterprise 640 *Zuleika* at sea week back in the sixties crewed by either Peter Tacon and Richard Fairburn. The conditions must have been pretty good, unlike today where no Ajax's or Squibs turned out. Tradition has it that a monetary prize would be given if a BOD ever capsized. I've not seen it take place in my life time but many have been sunk getting the main sheets wrapped around interesting objects.

Although the club premises have not changed much from my boyhood with their lovely paintings and photographs of a past era of sailing adorning the walls, it is the yacht basin that has seen so much change. Floating pontoons and gantries now give easy access to the yachts. In my time it was a case of rowing to your boat or calling the steward to come and get you. The sailing fleet has changed with the Dragons, an old Olympic class, virtually disappeared and being replaced mainly by BOD's. Clubs change and adapt and in this case, very much for the better.

40. Sea Week, Lowestoft

~ *Boswell's Broadland*

Patrick Boswell at the helm of *Smuggler*, crewed by Christine Boswell and Charles Bell

41. Somerton Staithe

Oil on board 10" x 8"

Location; Painted on the river bank between the old mill and Somerton village

Weather; Very bright and breezy with a strong westerly blowing

A very early start today arriving at about 8 am which gave me plenty of time for work but unfortunately the day took a long while to warm up. Surprisingly there were no holiday boats moored up apart from the sailing yacht *Swan* from Ludham. I painted her with her covers on as her crew were tucked up nicely inside out of the wind. Lucky things. The last time I came her by river was in terribly windy conditions with a group of other yachts and my outboard broke down in an isolated spot between here and Potter Heigham. Luckily, Peter Jeckells gave me a tow with *Moonraker* and saved the day.

At the end of the dyke, across the Horsey road, lives an old friend, Joe Bell. He once was the proud owner of a vintage steam launch called *Bubbles*. His son Charles used to crew us on *Smuggler* at the regattas and cruiser weekends. Charles worked for the Landamores at Wroxham fitting out electrics on the Oyster Yachts. Charles eventually went to the Carribean to see fame and fortune, settling down there in Trinidad and at one time managed a large yacht marina full of luxury boats, many of whom would over-winter there during the hurricane season. He is a rare visitor to these shores having a young family to look after.

My morning ended with coffee at Joe's. It was good to catch up on old times.

41. Somerton Staithe

~ *Boswell's Broadland*

42. Heigham Sound

Oil on board 11.5" x 9"

Location;Moored a few hundred metres from the turning to Horsey on a mud weight.

Weather; Dull day with the odd light shower. Wind south westerly, moderate.

For the first time for many weeks I am afloat with the help of a dory called *Raven* loaned by Patrick Richardson of Phoenix Fleet at Potter Heigham. The journey past Martham boatyard and left into Candle Dyke was pleasant enough with boats on the water first thing. I made good progress painting but as with these things it started to rain. Luckily I had my trusty William Cecil Hotel umbrella, loaned from Hillbrooke Hotels, with me. So I stood up painting and held the umbrella with my other hand. A bit wobbly but I managed it. I included *Black Bess*, a half-decker, in my painting as she looked very smart coming past. She was travelling quite fast so I had to alter the size of her in my painting before she disappeared around the corner. Because of the difficult conditions I decided to persevere with the weather and carry on rather than go home. I lifted my mudweight and headed for Horsey Mere.

42. Heigham Sound

~ *Boswell's Broadland*

43. Waxham New Cut

Oil on board 12" x 8"

H. Percival 1912
THE WHERRYMAN AND HIS WIFE

I was determined to revisit Waxham Dyke, tucked away in one corner of Horsey Mere but was surprised how far from its' mouth to the end of navigation it is. Its official title is Waxham New Cut but to me it looks like a very old bit of Broadland. Reeds have encroached on both sides and at one point I could nearly touch both sides. The water in the dyke is often a strong yellow or orange colour and I have been told it is caused by minerals from the close by sea seeping up into the fresh water of the Broads. Paul Bown, who I met in The Pleasure Boat Inn with his wife later that day, said he had seen a steady stream of the coloured water coming out into Horsey Mere at one time.

At the end of the dyke is a little bridge close to a boat yard that I didn't know existed. Standing on the river side you can see the bank close to Waxham beach and various caravan sites. More rain and it was definitely time to go and made the hour's journey back to Hickling to meet Patrick. It has been an interesting day starting with meeting Johnny Ladd, who had driven up early from Hastings to work on his sailing boat *Moth* which was looking very smart. He is a farmer who mills his own grain which is quite unusual these days. He told me about Ross Warrell who runs the *Lady Anne* day trip boat from Horsey and I was pleased to see him and his waving passengers on my journey. A quick beer in the pub and it was time for home.

43. Waxham New Cut

~ *Boswell's Broadland*

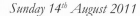

44. Hickling Village Regatta

Oil on board 18" x 12"

Location; At the end of the dyke by The Pleasure Boat Inn.

Weather; A bright, sunny day with cloud building. A warm breeze blowing down the Broad.

An early start from home gave me time to set up my easel and take in the beautiful panorama of Hickling Broad. The sailing club to my right with their dinghy park and on both sides of me in the dykes a real mix of half-deckers and Broads sailing cruisers.

Ross Warrell told me he set up the regatta at Hickling because the old style village one went into decline in the fifties. He and others had been running it for fourteen years now. It was nice to see a good fleet of keel boats on the Broad, out at one time.

My drawing and painting went well but, disaster, I had left my white spirit behind which I use to clean my brushes. Help was at hand as a kind man, Ray Harling, said he would go home and get me some. Such generosity. Coffee and cakes were taken at the W.I. tent and the river bank had a real carnival atmosphere with boats dressed overall and many were flying flags from their gaffs which is nice to see when they were racing. Winners medals for racing were even cast each year by Ross giving a unique memento of the days.

44. Hickling Village Regatta

~ *Boswell's Broadland*

45. The Hickling Pleasure Boat Inn

Oil on board 11" x9"

The pub, historically, goes back many centuries, standing in the corner of the Broad and was often used by wildfowlers. Prince Charles, as a young man, and his father stayed here on one such occasion and it was reported in the local paper. Nowadays the pub has recently gained freehold status and is run by Glynn giving it a new lease of life. It seems it is the local watering hole for a few people I haven't seen for years; Alan Tansley, Patrick and Jenny Simpson, back from their travels; and old friends Paul and Rosie Martin who keep their boat here.

I'm afraid the list goes on with Patrick Richardson and partner Carolyn with whom I found a table outside. Peter Jeckells arrived grandly in his vintage MG sports car and Robin, whose surname I can't recall, but owns that large forty foot Broads cruiser *Wood Nymph*. Our table was eventually completed by the arrival of Ian Pownall who used to run The Greyhound pub in the village but has subsequently been involved with his hog roast business for some years. This year he hopes to get the royal warrant for hog roast served at Sandringham on nine occasions. Oink oink.

All together a great day but it was time to slip away before I got too much in the party mood as I had to drive home. Didn't hear or see any bitterns on the broad but there was plenty of whooping and hollering coming from the pub.

45. Hickling Pleasure Boat Inn

~ *Boswell's Broadland*

No 3 of 20 a Norfolk Mill.   Chas. m. Wigg.

A NORFOLK MILL

Charles M. Wigg c1880

46. Horsey Staithe

Oil on board 15" x 12"

Location;At the end of Horsey Dyke adjacent to embarkation point for Ross River Trips.

Weather; Overcast with occasional sunny spells

This National Trust controlled estate owned by the Buxton family is the only broad with the title of 'mere'. I suppose it's because of its proximity to the sea. It was recently announced in the local papers that cranes had been successfully hatched and a small number have multiplied over the years. Quite a well kept secret. Conservation is the key here with the area being well managed and indeed visiting boats are discouraged in the winter months.

Ross Warrell and his family turned up to check on his boat which offers river trips and commentary on the wildlife. He later said he was going sailing which sounded fun. I had to continue working at what turned out to be a busy spot at the end of the dyke. It was nice to see a large proportion of sailing boats moored up here. It might have something to do with the high water levels as large motorised craft would not be able to navigate past Potter bridge.

I struggled a bit with my painting as the light conditions were ever changing but settled in the end for a low key element to my picture. On returning home I called in at both Martham Ferry and Martham Marine yards. The latter had an enormous amount of wooden vintage craft in the process of restoration. Quite a sight for *afficionados*.

46. Horsey Staithe

~ Boswell's Broadland

47. Womack Broad

Oil on board 14" x 12"

Location;On the green at Womack facing the staithe with boatyard and shops to the right.

Weather; Cloudy and a light breeze. Heavy rain in the afternoon.

This was nearly a day I didn't go painting as the forecast seemed so bad but I took my umbrella and I am glad I did. There was a mass of boats moored stern on at the staithe and people were very friendly. For such a small place Womack has a great deal of local history. The artist Edward Seago lived in The Dutch House backing on to the broad. It was from here he took his boats *Capricorn* and *Endeavour* on trips around The Broads as well as further afield, up the Seine to Paris and many coastal ports on the Continent. In particular Honfleur and Dieppe were immortalised by him.

Vaughan and Moira Ashby once ran their boatyard from here. Womack is home also to two famous boating centres. The Wherry Trust, where Norfolk's *Albion* was saved for the county and indeed was incidental in kickstarting marine conservation work throughout the country. Adjacent to these moorings is the home of The Hunter Fleet and yard. At one time owned and managed by Norfolk County Council to give youngsters a Broadland experience with their lovely varnished-hull sailing cruisers, they are now taken over by a trust. Both yards carrying a lovely aspect of Norfolk Broadland heritage. I hope to paint both yards at a later date and talk a little about their history. Mr. Martin Simms spoke to me at length about The *Albion* Wherry Trust and was most helpful about when I could paint.

As for my painting I focused on a superbly restored Broads motor cruiser *The Missouri Star* which was moored adjacent to a boatyard with its' adjoining shop Morris Marine run by Jacqui Morris. She was very friendly and asked to see my finished work. I had to laugh when one young lad with his father said my work was better than the child prodigy Keiron Williams. What could I say? I have been painting all my life and professionally for the last twenty years, but smile and say "thanks" without too much sense of sarcasm in my voice.

On completion I came home via Ludham Bridge Marine and hired a boat for Barton Regatta at the end of the month. It should be fun taking Christine's mother Marjorie for her first boating overnight experience.

47. Womack Broad

~ *Boswell's Broadland*

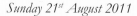

48. Oulton Regatta Week

Oil on board 16" x 11"

Location; In front of the Wherry Hotel with the panorama of the Broad in front of me.

Weather; Cloudy but warm day. A light westerly.

My memories of Oulton Week are peppered with strong winds and heavy downpours. Today however bucked the trend and I was glad I made an early start from home. Too early in fact, the first race was not until 10.00am. So I busied myself drawing and talking to holidaymakers. Most were enthusiastic and for the most part were on repeat Broadland holidays.

My memories of Oulton are of intense racing with my friends and much partying. I occasionally stayed on Tom Percival's parents' boat, sailing against their son. One time I had to borrow ten shillings from his mother for a protest against her own son. Tom won the protest and honour was duty bound for the Percival family. Tom went on to race at Oulton Broad with his powerboats when he was older. Bank holiday Monday was the day for the fair or the circus to be in Nicholas Everett Park next to the Waveney and Oulton Broad Clubhouse. At one time I witnessed tightrope walkers crossing the broad which was no mean feat. The powerboats would be stern-on to the quay heading by the Wherry Hotel and we all looked forward to one particular boat, *The Rooster*. I am pleased to say it has recently been restored after its heyday in the sixties. It is on display at Pleasurewood Hills Theme Park.

The regatta is the penultimate one in the Broadland calendar before Barton. Most of the sailing craft and support motor vessels leave on the Saturday before heading off on the long trip North.

My regatta journey is almost done but my Broadland trip goes on with a visit to St. Benet's Abbey tomorrow. I concluded my visit with a quick look in at the Oulton Broad Clubhouse and spoke briefly to David Yapp and John Ellis. David kindly introduced me to the commodore Will Smith who looked a bit apprehensive worrying about a fair breeze and dry weather , no doubt.

P.S. A seven year old said to me, 'Was I on the web as she would look me up?' Fame at last...

48. Oulton Regatta Week

~ *Boswell's Broadland*

49. St. Benet's Abbey

Oil on board 15" x 12"

Location; On the river bank close by the Abbey

Weather; Sunny with very little breeze

After turning off by The Dog PH at Ludham I eventually found my way to the Abbey. Initially I drove to Coldharbour which wasn't quite near enough but eventually found a little car park close by and it wasn't too much of an effort to find a nice spot by the river. The place has a serenity about it and one has to use imagination to re-member the Abbey as at one time it covered over thirty acres with a high wall encompassing places of worship, refectory and fish ponds in the grounds. Although Henry V111 did not demolish the abbey it has fallen into disrepair over the years, with only the gatehouse re-maining and a few of the outer walls. In the eigteenth century the brick base of a mill was incorporated on the site. A shame really.

The Bishop of Norwich, who is also the Bishop of St Benet's, comes once a year on the Wherry *Albion* to conduct a ceremony at this spot attended by many hundreds of followers.

In my painting, however, I wanted to portray a feeling of isolation and tranquillity. A bit difficult really with the fantastic sight of an army attack aircraft swooping low over me and following the con-tours of the river. I instantly gave him a wave but at that speed I hope he didn't wave back.

By mid-morning lots of boats had moored upstream from the Abbey with a few venturing over to see how I was getting on. One woman told me the scientific name for the storm flies stuck all over my picture. Thanks a lot. Home James and don't spare the fly spray.

49. St Benets Abbey

~ *Boswell's Broadland*

Thursday 25th August 2011

50. Ludham Bridge

Oil on board 15" x 12"

Location; Downstream from Ludham Bridge opposite Beta Marine and Ludham Bridge Boatyard

Weather; Unsettled with the occasional light shower. Heavy rain later.

I parked as close as I could to the bridge, collecting a coffee from the local cafe and had a quick browse around the boat sales area. They even had a Broads One Design for sale but it's out of my league at the moment.

There was quite a strong wind building up so I secured my easel down to avoid past disasters. The boatyard to the right is where I am hiring a small cruiser for the forthcoming Bank Holiday weekend. Christine's mother Marjorie who is 103 is coming along and I don't think she is too keen as she has never slept on a boat before.

The weather looks increasingly grim so I made haste with my picture. This is a busy spot for boats as the bridge allows only one through at any one time. There is usually a queue of boats waiting their turn. I showed one sailing boat negotiating the bend which was quite literally the only sailing vessel that passed by in several hours.

Job done and a quick chat to a local small boat owner who was moaning about the problems he has had with his engine. Oh the joys of boat ownership. He was at least kind enough about my painting. Home James as the heavens opened. Next week is Barton Regatta which I am looking forward to.

50. Ludham Bridge

~ *Boswell's Broadland*

Sunday 28th August 2011

51. Barton Regatta

Oil on board 18" x 12"

Location; Lee side of Barton Broad

Weather; Strong winds with heavy showers

A determination to stay on Barton Broad for the Regatta saw Christine and I together with aged mother hiring a cruiser from Ludham Bridge, towing *Wings*, my Norfolk dinghy alongside. The journey up the river Ant and through Irstead Shoals seemed to take forever with boats travelling nose to tail for miles. It was blowing pretty strongly so I moored behind the wherries *Albion* and *Solace* which proved to be a mistake as they kept dragging their moorings. In the end I sensibly went to the windward shore and moored up again.

As far as painting the regatta goes I don't think I did it justice. It was literally one hand for the boat and one for the painting. The light changed from bright sunlight to darkness with storm clouds overhead. I think it might be a case of re-jigging my effort later on in the studio.

A quick sail in *Wings* before supper of pork casserole followed by trifle. It doesn't get much better than that. Had a slight panic forgetting to pack the corkscrew but a nice man in a vintage gentleman's launch loaned me his.

Barton Broad has happy memories for me when I first took Christine sailing. She has been hooked ever since. As a boy my best friends were Peter and Anthony Sambrooke-Sturgess from nearby Neatishead Rectory. Their father, a Norwich dentist, was an expert on the international yacht racing rules. Being a family friend didn't cut any ice with him when I was involved with a racing protest with Reg Parsons, one time owner of *Madie*.

A quick 'hello' to Pat, Jenny and Ben Simpson and it was time for bed.

P.S Poor Beth broke her mast

Bank Holiday Monday 29th August 2011

Barton Broad Regatta,

I didn't paint today as my daughter Natalie and her husband James came along to join us. We picked them up from the staithe at Barton Turf by Cox's boatyard. They brought a lovely hamper of Coronation Chicken and pate and other yummy things. Natalie had made real millefuille which was delicious. I took them both out for a sail in *Wings* which they enjoyed, followed by a river tour down to Irstead Shoals to see the pretty thatched riverside houses, then back to Barton via Gay's Staithe. It is here that my father kept his old boat, *Catchalot*, in a nearby dyke. It was moored alongside an old house which had this arched tunnel running underneath it so a wherry could be drawn up and unloaded. I have not seen another of its' kind so I would consider it to be a unique building in Broadland.

Nearby was the old Barton Angler Hotel, now unfortunately turned into a private house. It was the scene of much jollity during regatta weekend when boat owners would decamp there for the amber nectar.

The weekend was unfortunately drawing to a close but I have enduring memories of a fabulously colourful scene. Literally hundreds of boats moored up either enjoying the atmosphere or waiting their turn to race. On the Norfolk Punt Club's pontoon the Wherry *Albion* moored up and had a brass band playing on board. The vintage steam launch 'Falcon' was busy ferrying passengers to and from the Museum of the Broads at Stalham. Many boats were dressed overall including four wherries; *Albion* and *Solace*, together with *Ardea* of Oulton and, I think, *White Moth*. *Ardea*, being returned from a mooring on the Seine in France and now fully restored to its' former glory. It brought back memories of my father's old wherry *Arcadia* as it had a very similar layout.

A wonderful regatta which I am sure will be thriving in generations to come.

P.S I gave a quick wave to John Aitken, Robert Self, Anthony Boardman and anybody else who would respond, as I sailed by. I was much amused by the lugsail dinghy sailed by Giles Bryan who was laying in the bottom of the boat unseen but had his faithful dog sitting upright in the stern and appeared to be steering on his own. The dog that is.

51. Barton Regatta

~ *Boswell's Broadland*

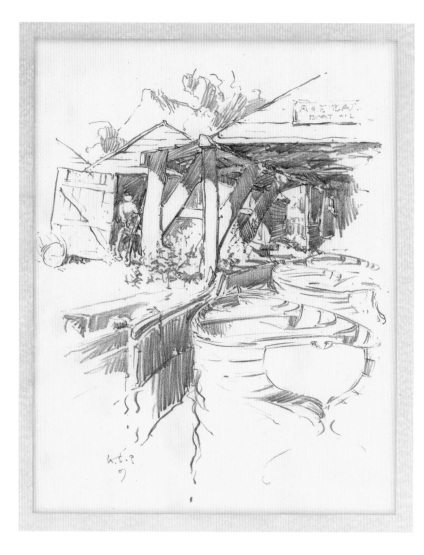

H. Percival 1907
A.J. BANHAM'S BOATYARD, HORNING

52. Cox's Boatyard, Barton Turf

Oil on board 16" x 8"

Location; A dyke beside Cox's boatyard

Weather; A warm day but at times overcast. A light north westerly breeze.

An early start to beat the traffic in Norwich and journeyed via Wroxham Bridge for a change, which wasn't too much of a bottleneck this time. Checking on *Wings* which lay by the staithe and spoke to a dear old man, John Yaxley, who worked for three generations of Landamores at Wroxham and had retired nearly twenty years ago. He much admired my boat and wanted to know where it had been built. We talked about his work which during the war was spent working on lifeboats and fast harbour and coastal vessels.

Time marched on so I made haste to the yard which has a large row of dilapidated boat sheds due for demolition and redevelopment. I wanted to commit them to canvas before they disappeared. They have planning approval to turn them into apartments with wet boat docks underneath according to the yard manager Eric Bishop. He was most helpful and we talked about Tim Cox, who I went to school with and previously owned the yard , sadly not living next door any more. Fond memories of Tim and my sailing friends who attended discos and barbeques in these sheds for quite a few regattas in the sixties.

My eventual painting position was in front of the solar powered vessel called *Ra*, named after the Sun God. The boatsheds were a great subject to paint with few interuptions apart from one of Cox's men, Josh Bridges. I said "That's a good old Broadland name". "Actually," he said "I'm from Dover". Another man invited me onto his boat to look at a picture he had bought from a car-boot sale of a sailing galleon. Surprisingly my painting went well and I was at a loss whether to continue here or go on my way. The latter prevailed.

52. Cox's Boatyard, Barton Turf

~ *Boswell's Broadland*

53. The Horning Swan Inn and Wherry Albion

Oil on board 15" x 12"

After a bit of a detour to find a possible painting spot at Irstead Shoals I ended up in Horning by The Swan. It was on my list of paintings to do so I set to with speed. The Wherry *Albion* was moored up with a large party aboard. The skipper kindly told me they were there for one and a half hours. My picture had mixed success as it really was a painting of two halves. The Swan on one side and the wherry on the other. I put a few people in to help link the halves together. This is a very busy spot so there was a constant "That's well good" from youngsters, with the occasional "wicked" thrown in.

The Swan itself was built in 1897 and is not that old in real terms and, I suppose, was built to cater for the large numbers of holidaymakers coming to the Broads at the turn of the century. The railways had opened up Norfolk and Horning was a thriving boat hire centre with Percivals, Southgates and Banhams all thriving. A lot of these yards have been turned into riverside developments in the past thirty or so years.

It was at this spot on the river green, by The Swan, where a lot of the scenes of *Swallows and Amazons*, the film, took place. My father's boat, *Catchalot*, was hired and was steered by Sam Kydd with father inside the cabin given instructions. Two other friends provided boats. Pat Simpson loaned the *Death and Glory* which was crewed by the Dimbleby twins. Pat Richardson loaned his boat *Buttercup* for scenes, I believe, filmed on South Walsham Broad. A great time was had by all but sadly I was away working in London so could not join in the fun.

The Swan lawn was a good place to stand on a windy Saturday afternoon because the novice yacht hirers, coming down from Wroxham usually on a broad reach with sail fully extended would not know as they turned the corner that the boom would come crashing across, sending them completely out of control, much to the delight of onlookers finishing their pints.

The river between The Swan and the Ferry Boat Inn is a notoriously sheltered spot and is known locally as The Street. Many a race has been won or lost here as yachts wend their way back from downriver races from Thurne Mouth or returning on the Three Rivers race in the middle of the night.

C. M. Wigg
THE FISHING MATCH, HORNING

53. The Swan Inn at Horning and the Wherry, 'Albion'

~ *Boswell's Broadland*

54. How Hill

Oil on board 15" x 12"

Location; On the staithe at How Hill adjacent to the moorings for the Electric Eel rivercraft.

Weather; A dull day at first but the sun broke through by lunchtime.

Today was the second time that I was accompanied by my artist friend Paul Darley. I arranged to pick him up from the station at Wroxham as he was coming in from Cromer.

We walked up and down the river bank until eventually settling on a view upstream with the *Electric Eel* thatched boat house and the skeleton old wind pump in the middle distance. This is a seriously busy place with dozens of boats moored up together as well as cyclists and visitors to the How Hill centre passing by. On the river I spoke to Paul Bown sailing a half decker which I believe is a Yarmouth rater, sail no H/2. He was soon gone heading for Ludham Bridge but was quickly replaced by youngsters rowing half-deckers and Hustler yachts being quanted with great gusto by hearty souls.

After talking to numerous holiday makers, who took photographs of me, I decided to look in at the charming Toad Hall Cottage close by. It was formerly an eel catchers dwelling. It is hard to appreciate that at one time the marshman and his six or seven children, lived here cramped into a two bed cottage. Cooking was on an open fire and they probably lived quite well from their small kitchen garden, supplemented by rabbits, fish and wildfowl from the marshes. The garden is planted with herbs today to illustrate their importance in daily life for curing coughs and colds. I like sage grown for white teeth, hair tonic; and wormwood for expelling internal worms. In the larder of the cottage there is a display of old marshman's tools with lovely names like crome, twitchrake, rabbiting spade, dydle and hodder, whatever they all are.

By lunchtime Paul had finished a good rendition of the *Albion* as she sailed by and I too had completed my task. It was time for home and a quick cup of tea and cake at Ludham Bridge before dropping Paul at the Wroxham train station.

54. How Hill

~ *Boswell's Broadland*

55. Irstead Shoals

Oil on board 15" x 12"

Location; Moored upstream from The Shoal's House

Weather; Warm but cloudy start becoming sunny later. A light southerly breeze.

Today I made a determined effort to take *Wings* out and paint from her. The weather was good and all I had to do was push her into the water from the grassy bank at Barton Staithe.

It was at this point that I met David Collins-Cubitt who kindly took my photo, for the record.

I met Beth and Lesley and others who were in a small flotilla of half-deckers and sailing cruisers hired from Hunters Yard. Apparently they were part of a sailing club set up some twenty five years ago by Val and Neville at The Horstead Centre near Coltishall. It was inspired by Arthur Ransomes' Coot Club book and exists to this day getting youngsters out on the water handling traditional sailing craft. They looked as if they were having fun, even sleeping aboard a couple of half deckers. One young girl, sailing her Tideway (*Dipper*), said "hi" and that she used to be a Frostbite winter sailing club member sailing aboard Norfolk dinghy no 53 *Twinkle*. I later twigged that she was Erica Chisholm as her face seemed very familiar. She works away now but kindly sent me more details on the 'Coots Unleashed' which she has run since 2008, keeping up the spirit of the original concept that Val and Neville started. For one week every summer they sail off in half-deckers from Hunter's Yard and spend their days exploring the Broads and the evenings sleeping on the boats under awnings.

I was determined not to use my electric outboard and headed out to the broad single-handed. By 9.00am I was tacking across Barton Broad with the place pretty much to myself. Just beyond the far neck of the broad lies Irstead Shoals and I mud-weighted onto an alder bank together with a further mudweight aft to adjust my position. I concentrated on painting the lovely thatched house on the bend of the river, which I believe is unoccupied at the moment. It is a lovely house with bedrooms and balconies on the first floor and with wet boat shed beneath.

The house next door has a chandelier hanging in its wet boat shed. That's decadence for you.

Painting progressed well and I waved to interested passers-by. After packing up I had the benefit of a great downwind run back across the broad with the wind picking up slightly. Half an hour later *Wings* was put to bed for the day and I was sadly making my way home after a great day on the water.

55. Irstead Shoals

~ *Boswell's Broadland*

56. Neatishead Village

Oil on board 12" x 10"

Location; In the centre of the village facing The White Horse Inn and Ye Olde Saddlery Restaurant

Weather; A cloudy day with strong westerly winds

Within moments of setting up my easel I got speaking to an elderly gentleman called Teddy whose cottage I was standing in front of. He had been living there some years. His neighbour from across the road, Richard Thompson, offered me a cup of tea which was sent by his wife Irene. This was only the second cuppa offered in fifty pictures so I was most grateful. Richard told me about the village sign having three shields; depicting the Preston family, local gentry since the eighteenth century; the second shield represents its connection with St Benets Abbey before the Reformation; the last shield its association with RAF Neatishead radar station. This tragically some years ago, was the site of an underground fire in which several firemen perished in the smoke logged tunnels beneath. Very sad .

The ancient spelling of Neatishead amused me and is spelt 'Inetshead' . The start of the word is how young people today illiterate their speech, 'Init?' Richard said the word was from the Anglo-Saxon period and could mean a pile of offal. Offally nice init?

Sally Spall stopped her car and said 'hello' which was a nice surprise.

As a young man I stayed with the Sambrooke-Sturgess family at Barton Rectory close by. No electricity then with Mrs Sturgess' bantams coming in and out of the kitchen. Bedtime necessitated a candle in a holder or a flickering Tilly lamp. Very *Swallows and Amazons*.

I had only painted a small panel this time and was soon on my way to Barton Staithe to check on *Wings*. It was her 80th birthday on Sunday but I forgot to bring any flowers. Tough luck is what I say.

P.S. Just spotted at Neatishead a 'Boswell's Cottage'. They really should not have named it so soon after my visit. Fame at last.

56. Neatishead Village

~ *Boswell's Broadland*

57. Wayford Bridge

Oil on board 10" x 8"

It was not far along the back roads to Wayford Bridge and I was glad the weather was still holding but with the wind increasing.

There are two boatyards here and I painted on the river bank closest to the bridge. There was virtually no river traffic apart from the odd day launch hired from the opposite river bank. The area I was painting in is a vast arena of yachts and motor boats in various degrees of restoration. Quite quiet today thronging at the weekend with enthusiastic boat restorers no doubt. I wonder how many of these projects will ever bear fruit. If I was younger I would have a go myself but like to think I have a slightly wiser head on me now and can see the months of sanding and replacing timbers that these old craft need.

My easel started to take off a couple of times so speedily finished painting in record time. If I get any faster I will bring a new meaning to the word 'Impressionism'.

Before I forget there is a long dyke that exits the river by John Royall's house and is the final resting place of my father's old wherry *Arcadia*. Towed to the end of the dyke into one of those flooded marshy areas and has sunk without much evidence of it still existing. I went there some years back and I think I could make out the rough outline of her with tufts of grass and debris marking her final resting place. Gone but not forgotten.

C. M. Wigg
(possibly Hunsett)

57. Wayford Bridge

~ *Boswell's Broadland*

58. Dilham Tonnage Bridge

Oil on board 10" x 8"

Location; On the public staithe at Dilham

Weather; Warm and cloudy with very little breeze

Started about 9.00am and had the place pretty much to myself apart from one hire cruiser overnighting by the bridge. David and Jan Lock, the hirers, said the sunset last night was superb with the bridge being lit up with the dying sun's rays. David said it was their first Broads holiday and they seemed to be enjoying themselves. In the past they had taken boating holidays on the French canals with Horizon. He described some of the rise and fall of the lock systems was a bit scary for the novice. At any rate his boat, *Little Gem*, soon departed heading back through Wayford Bridge to his hirers yard. There is a very high water table at the moment and they only cleared the bridge by a matter of inches. Potter Bridge can not be navigated at the moment.

A lovely spot here which I must admit I have only visited once before with *Smuggler*. This is the end of navigation as the other side of the bridge is the disused North Walsham and Dilham canal. The canal is under restoration at the moment.

Dilham is well known to me as my sister Anne lived there for some time at The Old Stables, and Sir Robert Carr, a distant relative, lived close by at the Smallburgh entrance to the village. John and Kate Aitken have a house here and moorings which I have visited in the past. John and Kate are the only people that I know who once owned a house that had a fake fibreglass brick effect garden wall, installed by a film company. They liked it so much they left it in situ. John's father was the Bishop of Kings Lynn retiring to Ranworth so the whole family had big Broadland boating connections including Kate, who was from the famous Eastwood boating dynasty.

Apart from the painting I waited to make a telephone bid for two C.M. Wigg etchings at G.A. Key's auctioneers, of Broadland subjects for which I am pleased to say I was successful.

58. Dilham Tonnage Bridge

~ *Boswell's Broadland*

C. J. Watson
ACLE July 14th 1888

59. Sutton Staithe

Oil on board 11" x 9"

I parked close by the Sutton Staithe Hotel and proceeded to set up my easel facing the end of the dyke and the Sutton Staithe boatyard run by Robert Frearson. A kind lady in the office answered my questions about the old RNLI lifeboat depicted in the centre of my painting undergoing restoration. It was built in 1924 and served for fifty years in the North Sea. Its original name was *King of Prussia*.

It was quite a nice spot here with holiday craft continually mooring up on their way into Stalham across the busy road or heading for the hotel. Close by is Richardson's Boatyard, one of the biggest hirers on the Broads. Not far also from the Museum of the Broads which I hope to visit later.

59. Sutton Staithe

~ *Boswell's Broadland*

60. Museum of the Broads

Oil on board 13" x11"

Location; Inside the boat shed at the museum

Weather; Overcast to start with but sunny after mid-morning. Gale force winds.

The museum lies in an attractive part of Broadland with little dykes leading on to the main river. Patrick Simpson's old yard is just around the corner on one side and an old tall milling building on the other. Many of the houses in this mini village have undergone restoration in recent years, so the museum sits well within its environment.

I was a little like a kiddy in a sweet shop. There was so much to see and do ably helped by the museum staff. I had a free hand to paint where I pleased and wandered through the exhibits learning so much about Broadland that I knew only in outline. There are sections on the Broads at war, the story of the holiday industry, the life of old marshmen and wherrymen and sections on the origins of the Broads. Even Roman life has a mention. It was nice to see a good section on Tom Percival, Norfolk's international power boat champion. His father and grandfather were in the boat business as H.T.Percival of Horning and his mother was from the famous Brooke Marine boat building family of Oulton Broad. They were founding members of the Oulton Broad power boat club.

I chose the 'Boat Shed' to paint inside because of the historical boats within. The pride of the museum is the one hundred and eighty year old racing yacht *Maria* which is believed to be the oldest of its kind in the country still in its original condition.

To the left is the immaculate BOD 'dabchick' no 6, owned by Sir Timothy Colman. The room is peppered with other interesting artefacts and boats. There is a lifeboat which was dropped by air to downed airmen in the Channel and Atlantic seas, an early Norfolk sailing punt and numerous wooden canoes and dinghys.

Standing and painting by the door, visitors thought I was part of the staff there and kept asking me questions, which was quite funny. Even a blind man with his audio link wanted to know where no 10 was and how many steps.

Not a problem to finish and I was soon back looking around. I expressed an interest in the old enamel badges that boatyards gave their holiday hirers, of which I have a good collection. The staff gave me some further information on boatyard pennants. I am always quizzing my friend Mike Powles, from the Powles boatyard family at Wroxham, if he had found a badge for me from his old family business. It has a red circle and blue star. Some names are gone from the Broadland scene but a list of the old yards included Moores, Loynes, Allens, Martham, Hipperson, Turners, Collins, Banhams, Powles and the Norfolk Broads Yachting Co. Museum staff told me that a museum friend had sent a collection of Broadland badges through the post which had got lost. I will have to see if I can help them out when the time comes.

Punch-drunk with images of days gone by, I couldn't find anything on the family *Arcadia*, but shall keep delving. A great place to visit for a few hours or take a trip in the steam launch *Falcon*, named after the Lacons Brewery family's logo. I think one of my favourite objects in the museum is the old bar made in the shape of a boat by H. T. Percival of Horning and at one time decorated the Ranworth Malsters pub. Many a time I have propped this up in my youth.

60. Museum of the Broads

~ *Boswell's Broadland*

61. Hunter's Fleet, Womack

Oil on board 16" x 11"

Location; At Hunters Yard looking back at the two boatsheds.

Weather; A beautifully sunny day but still with a keen south westerly wind blowing.

As a 'Friend of Hunters Fleet' it was nice to feature it in my painting and do my little bit to keep these lovely old sailing boats afloat. For those of you not familiar with the boats they were originally founded by Percy Hunter and his sons Cyril and Stanley at the turn of the 20ᵗʰ century. Norfolk County Council saved them from being sold off as motor cruisers became the norm on the Broads. They were then used for sail training but as things turned out the yard was once again put up for sale but was saved for the county by countless individual donations to form the Norfolk Heritage Fleet Trust.

I have never sailed one of these boats. The cruisers do not have engines and their crew are reliant upon muscle power and a quant when the wind drops. Bryan Read, their chairman, kindly sent me a badge together with the fleet history. It's funny how family and events become interlinked, as I discovered on reading that my son-in-law, James Mead, is the Grandson of Ian Coutts who once owned Rebel *Reveller* now restored and in the fleet. Ian was at one time chairman of Norfolk County Council. I do intend to have a sail in her one day and to take all the family.

The yard was quite quiet today as most of the fleet was out on hire. It must have been a block booking as I saw a whole gaggle of them as I passed over Potter Bridge.

Tim Frary kindly gave me permission to paint. Later on I spoke to Vikki Walker, the manageress for the past five years, and she told me the names of the other men working today; John Franks and Derryl Jay. She said that there are five and-a-half people employed which made me smile. I think the half person was the man working in the office, a keen collector of old Broadland books. Aren't we all?

H.Percival

My painting position was next to the sailing yacht *Kenmure* owned by B. Eddy sail no 257. They kindly gave me a cup of tea which was very welcome considering, although sunny the wind was quite biting. The painting went well so I was able to take in the scene which is a delightful spot not far from Womack Staithe and access to Thurne Mouth just close by. I watched a group of lads opposite with an Eastwood Whelpton boat struggling to put in reefs before setting off for Barton. They prudently motored out of the dyke before setting sail on the main river. A quick cheerio to the very helpful yard staff and off to my next location next door.

61. Hunter's Fleet, Womack

~ *Boswell's Broadland*

62. The Wherry Trust, Ludham

Oil on board 15" x 12"

C. M. Wigg
BARTON BROAD

Too nice to head for home so I was glad to have another fantastic subject close by. The wherries *Maud* and *Albion* were tucked into their mooring and wet shed. I was previously led to believe that they normally would have left their home base by 9.30am but I expect either the strong winds or no group bookings have kept them at home. Because, as boats, they are complicated to paint it helped that their masts were stepped and that nobody was aboard moving about to disturb my view.

In the small dyke behind me were two river commissioners' launches getting ready to go out. They, in turn, lay on the boundary of Colin Buttifant 's yard. On the other side of the Wherry Trust's dyke is the Broads Authority's depot for Broadland maintenance. There were a serious amount of vehicles in the yard getting ready for the days work out on the marshes, banks and other locations.

Beside the wherry's wet dock is a large wooden building which I suppose houses all the sundry equipment to run these lovely vessels and a useful place to give visiting parties safety boat instructions for the day ahead.

Very tired now but glad I took the time to do a second painting today. Not much detail but I hope I captured the spirit of them.

62. The Wherry Trust, Ludham

~ *Boswell's Broadland*

63.Hunsett Mill

Oil on board 16" x 11"

Location; Downstream from Hunsett Mill where I mudweighted Wings.

Weather; Sunny day with light easterly winds

I had a feeling today was going to be a challenging one. The old adage 'fail to prepare and prepare to fail ' stood true. I had checked the weather forecast with light winds from the east so I could easily sail *Wings* in both directions to the mill without tacking. The reality was, of course, the wind was non existent so I paddled there and back taking nearly an hour each way. My trusty electric outboard lay languishing in my studio.

Having previously reconnoitred and getting no response from the Mill's owners, as yet by email, for permission to paint on their river bank I moored *Wings* as close as I could on a mud weight, sticking out a bit into the river. Luckily, very little traffic seemed to be coming past. A yacht loaned from the NBYC company shouted out that I deserved ten out of ten for effort, painting from my little boat. Just like being at school. Various canoeists came past taking photos and chatting away. I asked one gentleman, who I must say was a bit on the large side, if he was team-building. "No" was his response, "just trying to stay upright". He did look a bit unsteady.

For some unknown reason I left *Wings'* sails up, partly out of laziness as it gave me a little more headroom for painting. The sun was beating down on my back and I was glad when the sails swung my way to give me a little shade. An elderly gentleman sailing solo in a hired craft drifted past so I just about managed to get him in the picture. If it had been a studio picture, a quick series of snaps would probably have resulted in a better composition. He was soon gone.

The Mill and cottage are quite well known to my family as my sister Anne was once married to Christopher Sands who owned all the land around here and back towards Wayford Bridge as well. He told me that after the war the cottage was once occupied by Winston Churchill's private secretary. The cottage has now doubled in size with a remarkable wooden building with black tarred boarding and an amazing sloping ridge to the roof. Quite contemporary and, I gather, has won several architectural awards. I loved it. I am sure plenty of people would disagree.

63. Hunsett Mill

~ *Boswell's Broad;and*

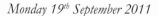

H. Percival, 1921
HARVESTING

64. South Walsham Broad

Oil on board 15" x 12"

Location; On the quay heading of Russell Marine

Weather; A sunny day but with low temperatures to start with

South Walsham is a pretty Broad with its shoreline of thatched houses, but from my perspective not much access for an artist. The local council have beautifully restored a slipway on the village staithe but this gave me a limited view of the Broad.

I approached Rod Russell of Russell Marine who could not have been more helpful with his boatyard having commanding views of the broad. A steady shuttle of holiday boats came and moored up for water and fuel and most were complimentary about my painting, one making me pose for a photo.

I know the broad well because it is one of the destinations for the Three Rivers Race, often navigated in the dark. An episode of *Swallows and Amazons* was also filmed here with lots of local 'in period' boats taking part to various degrees.

On completion of my painting Rod showed me work he had underway. There is a lovely 1930's motor cruiser *Fanny Ann* built originally by Brooke Marine. It is one of those ones with a glazed structure on the hull giving all round visibility. She will look lovely when completed. In the shed was a very large 1950's cruiser nearing completion called 'F.O.B' of Great Yarmouth. She was built by Powles of Wroxham and when originally constructed was taken from the patterns that were for the launches of the Royal Yacht Britannia.

Rod told me that a local artist, Chris Springham, had restored an old Victorian skiff, *Laura II*, and had it launched with a party of people dressed in Victorian clothing. Sadly he passed away recently.

A most interesting morning was spent and it was time to make my farewells and onward to Ranworth.

64. South Walsham Broad

~ *Boswell's Broadland*

Frank Gillet
RATCATCHER

To Chris Helsham
3rd T.P.

Frank Gillett

65. Ranworth Staithe

Oil on board 11" x 9"

Ranworth village is always a delight to visit when you approach from the Acle or Upton directions by road. Down the hill is the Old Maltsters PH and quayside is the Poplars shop and Wildlife Visitors Centre . The Centre gave me helpful tips about the Broad and I could have taken time to go to the floating platform centre for a commanding view of Ranworth Broad. I decided against this because of time pressure so set up my easel on the staithe.

It's a bit confusing, the Broad here is called Malthouse but the staithe is Ranworth with Ranworth Broad proper not noticeable from this point. Boat hirers cannot go there as it is a wildlife conservation area. In the background of my picture is Ranworth Church which, if you are of sound mind and heart, has magnificent views from its tower. I imagine Yarmouth and Norwich could be spotted on a clear day. Too much for me! The church itself has one of the finest rood screens in the country having survived the Reformation.

Ranworth Country Club lies close by and using the word 'rude ' again with a different spelling was the scene of many a jolly evening in my youth for, shall we say, 'exotic' cabarets. I recall one particular evening, the young lady did not turn up and faced with angry punters the resourceful owners wife duly stepped into the breach, so to speak. Some years later my father looked at the club when looking for a business venture for his retirement. He, in the end, settled for The Royal Hotel at Mundesley, where I met 'her indoors' (Christine), so it was a good move on his part.

I suspect Ranworth, at the weekends, gets pretty packed so I am glad I saw her on a sunny day at her best without too many visitors.

65. Ranworth Staithe

~ *Boswell's Broads*

C. M. Wigg
HORNING FERRY

66. Horning Ferry Inn

Oil on board 12" x 10"

Location; Opposite bank to The Ferry Inn

Weather; Sunny spells with a light south westerly breeze.

It was my daughter Natalie's birthday so after an early start to drop off presents I was on my way via Woodbastwick. I had never been down that road to the river and so was uncertain if I could get close enough to the river to paint. The road was slightly flooded but not to any great depth. There were only a few cruisers on the river bank as the bulk of boats had moored up at The Ferry Inn opposite for food and drink. The pub itself in recent times has had a bit of a chequered career with closures from time to time but is still a popular destinations for locals as well. During the war the pub took a direct hit from a German bomber killing many of the customers and airmen from RAF Coltishall nearby. Rumour had it that Douglas Bader had left the pub not long before it was bombed. At any rate it's in fine fettle now and was a good subject to paint standing proudly on a bend in the river on the edge of Horning. No ferry now operates but launches can be hired by ringing the boatyard opposite.

There is a large metal statue opposite of a heron, known locally as Harry, gaining some notoriety by being erected without planning permission by the Funnell boatyard. I think I was painting in his favourite spot because a heron came in to land where I was but changed his mind at the last moment. Picture finished and as the day brightened I headed for a new location.

66. Horning Ferry Inn

~ *Boswell's Broads*

68. Salhouse Broad

Oil on board 15" x 12"

My cousin Christine who lives in Australia knew that I was painting the broad and was keen to see my Salhouse effort. I didn't realise that the distance to the water's edge was so far. My equipment was heavy but the way was very well maintained both in gravel and boardwalk. In fact I learned that the broad was dug for gravel extraction and then flooded by rising water levels, unlike the rest of the Broads being excavated for their peat content.

After finding a charming spot to paint with manicured grassy banks I met the Broads Ranger Tobi Baker who was most helpful offering me a trip across the river to Hoveton Great Broad, a wildlife conserved area. A keen collector of Broads books, he showed interest in my painting and said he would look out for my Broadland book if it ever gets published. Oh ye of little faith.

The land and Broad here are owned and managed by the Cator family. Henry Cator, I gather, fell off his bike and broke his wrist recently. Infinitely better than falling off his perch I should think.

As midday passed it clouded over and made painting difficult so I headed back along the quarter of a mile path. It's been a long day.

67. Salhouse Broad

~ *Boswell's Broadland*

68. Hoveton Little Broad

Oil on board 12" x 6"

Location; Bottom of garden of Run Cottage by the Broad

Weather; Misty start with sun burning through mid morning

I knew I would have difficulty finding a view of the broad because access is only from the Horning to Wroxham road side of the water which is mostly under private ownership. A nice man walking an unruly puppy near an adjacent boatyard suggested I tried further up by the little bridge and try and walk through the reed bed. This really was impractical so I knocked on the door of Run Cottage and the owners, Ray Underwood and his wife, kindly gave me permission to paint at the bottom of their garden. It didn't provide me with a clear view of the broad but was, none the less, OK for my purposes. It was very misty to start with and I think I could just make out the only entrance to the broad from the River Bure. Many years ago this entrance was locked in winter time and local boat owners took it upon themselves to break open the barrier to give continual access to the broad. This action, I believe, took place in the fifties/sixties and resulted in quite a lot of discussion in the local papers. There is always a fine line between continual public access and private waters.

As a boy I sailed my Enterprise here with the Horning Sailing Club running races from time to time. It was a tricky place to sail on as the wind eddies around the hill on one side and trees on the other. Tom Percival and I had many a battle here with him invariably winning. Andy Fisher and his brother Beverly lived in one of the grand houses overlooking the Broad. I think it was called Little Crabbets and they joined in the racing together with the Mallands and the Paceys, all keen members.

To me this broad has a charm of its own and today was no exception. I always refer to it as Black Horse Broad though the pub bearing this name has long been demolished to make way for housing.

Onwards to my next destination.

C. M. Wigg, 1926

68. Hoveton Little Broad

~ *Boswell's Broadland*

69. Wroxham Bridge

Oil on board 14" x 12"

C. A. Hannaford
MASTER MARINERS

Parking is always an issue in Wroxham with the village still busy with late Broadland holidaymakers. Luckily the Hotel Wroxham, at one time owned by the Trafford family and probably still is, gave me permission to paint on their dyke quayheading and park close by. I was a little too close to the bridge to get the best position to paint but really had no other choice because of the large numbers of boats mooring up or just passing under the bridge. The old bridge has a modern pedestrian walkway attached to it so making the original piered and stone structure slightly obscured. Broadland artists have painted this fine bridge throughout the ages from Leslie Moore to Arthur Davies and I am joining them. At one time it had a tall wooden mill-like structure close by and was a mooring place for wherries to unload and drop their counterweight masts. My father's old wherry *Arcadia* was once wintered here for running repairs.

Wroxham itself with Roys stores dominates the village and is credited with being the largest village store in the world with shops of all descriptions in the centre. One shop owner, Gary Rodgers, of Broads Newsagents, came and had a chat and expressed an interest in my work which was nice to hear. He said his son worked for Waterstones at the UEA.

A blisteringly hot day now and I was glad to pack up after a day well spent. For the last few days I have been in London visiting Design shops and a quick trip to Wiltshire to see my daughter Sophie and her fiancée Ryan. All this travelling is getting pretty exhausting.

69. Wroxham Bridge

~ *Boswell's Broadland*

70. Wherry Yacht Charter Trust Base, Hoveton

Oil on board 12" x 13"

Location; The Wherry base in Hartwell Road, Wroxham, at Barton House Cottage.

Weather; Sunny day with southerly winds.

It is not often that I am completely taken aback by something but the setting of the base at Wroxham in the grounds of Peter Bowers home is quite idyllic. He is a railway enthusiast and has built a small guage railway in his garden together with buildings to house his collection of railway memorabilia. One building is the old signal box from Honing. On the river bank are railway signs 'Riverside East and West'.

I was met by Chris Matthews who I used to work with as a humble laminator at Aquafibre, Rackheath where Chris was a highly skilled mould-maker. The firm was one of the forerunners of the GRP laminating business and they, I believe, built or fitted out the hull for Ted Heath's *Morning Cloud*, as one of their projects. Chris showed me around all the wherries now being restored with the benefit of Heritage Lottery Funding. The boats are housed in a purpose built tented structure over a quay headed dyke which can house the three boats comfortably. The *Hathor* and *Olive* need urgent repair and the *Norada* is under restoration. The *Hathor* has a fascinating background being commissioned by the Colman family and named after the goddess of love and joy. Jeremiah Colman had a son, Alan, who went to Egypt to try and cure his tuberculosis with the dry climate. They journeyed on the *Hathor of Luxor* down the Nile but Alan sadly succumbed to the disease. The wherry when launched was named after this sad episode in their family life.

The inside of the boat is decorated with symbols of Egyptian hieroglyphics and interiors designed by Edward Boardman, the up and coming architect, who had married into the family.

The guys I met are mostly volunteers and Chris told me his brother Barney was one of the owners of *Norada*. I have taken the trouble to list them as they looked after me so well with tea and even a glass of wine. Robert Boswell (no relative), Chris Matthews, as mentioned, Mervyn Edge (gardener), Jake Stock, apprentice, Tim Waters and Andy Beaumont, also an artist I believe.

I decided to paint an upright picture this time because the space determined where I could stand. On reflection I should have just painted a small section of these very large boats. Perhaps another time. If ever there is a fund-raising event, do visit these wonderful old boats or go out and charter them when they are restored.

H. Percival

70. Wherry Yacht
Charter Trust base
~ *Boswell's Broadland*

71. Belaugh Village

Oil on board 10" x 8"

Location; Lower Street Belaugh by the staithe

Weather; Cloudy and very windy, north westerly

After a day in Stamford at The William Cecil Hotel hanging over one hundred and fifty pictures I was in two minds about painting today. With this being the penultimate painting of my Broadland odyssey I just had to make the effort. It was very windy and a there was a definite autumnal feel to the day.

Belaugh is a lovely village and houses nestle by the church with their lawned gardens going down to the river. The staithe is in The Street, well actually the adjacent street, as far as I could see. It was difficult to get a good view of the river because of the trees but with the church on the hill in the background and Belaugh's only boatyard viewed through the trees, I think I pulled it off. Definitely no time to hang around and I think a little retouching back in the studio would be called for this time.

On returning home I called in at the Wroxham boat auction run by Irelands and spoke briefly to Robin Richardson of Phoenix Fleet and one of the guys from The Wherry Trust Restoration team. I resisted buying anything.

71. Belaugh Village

~ *Boswell's Broadland*

72. Coltishall Village Green

Oil on board 11" x 9"

Journeys end today and I have foregone painting the two pubs that I know well, The Rising Sun and The Kings Head but faced the other way towards the two thatched buildings on the green.

Coltishall is a very pretty village and was known in the past as having the oldest boatyard, Allens, for building wherries. The last one was in 1921 called *Ella*. The yard closed in 1974. The green itself is surprisingly owned by Kings College, Cambridge. Like a lot of old villages rumour and superstition were rife. Old Shuck the wild dog is supposed to roam these parts and if you were to meet him on the old bridge superstition had it that you would die within the year. Anne Boleyn's father was also supposed to carry his daughter's head under his arm across the bridge on her birthday. Can't say I have noticed him.

After a quick drink at The King's Head run by Mrs Sue Gardener to celebrate my epic journey I bade farewell to The Broads for the moment. Many happy memories of wonderful people I have met along my way.

P.S. Not many people know this but the originator of Bob the Builder was brought up here at The King's Head. His parents once showed me his sketch book before he went to art school and I was sceptical that he would make is as an artist. He is now a multi-millionaire and I have egg on my face. Well done, the boy done great!

72. Coltishall Village Green

~ Boswell's Broadland

73. Wherries Yarmouth bound

~ Boswell's Broadland